Communication in Drama:

A Pragmatic Approach

Dr. Umesh S. Jagadale

PARTRIDGE
A Penguin Random House Company

To order additional copies of this book, contact
Partridge India
000 800 10062 62
orders.india@partridgepublishing.com

www.partridgepublishing.com/india

Contents

KEY TO ABBREVIATIONS AND SYMBOLS

Abbreviations:

s	=	Speaker
h	=	Hearer
G	=	Goal
u	=	Utterance
ri	=	Rising Intonation
fi	=	Falling Intonation
P	=	Pause
sd	=	Stage Direction
n	=	Negation

Symbols:

' / '	=	rising intonation
' \ '	=	falling intonation

PREFACE

*C*ommunication in Drama: *A Pragmatic Approach* is a book dedicated to study the 'say' and 'play' of all possible communicators operating the process of communication in drama. The pragmatic approach adopted here facilitates to explore, investigate and explain the dynamics of communication in drama. The book refers to five Indian plays in English, as also to some other plays and one-act-plays in this endeavor. Since the communication in drama has situational dynamism, it becomes essential to focus on the speech situations in drama while undertaking a study of this kind. The speech situations in drama are formed and operated by several elements. Moreover, the sets and subsets of the elements often do vary from situation to situation. The very identification of the presence and function of these elements is the first and foremost riddle to solve. Evans (1985) indicates the dynamism in the forming and functioning of the speech situations in drama as follows:

> *The situation contains much more than what we observe. As though obeying the law of plentitude, it contains all the objects that are there, and all their properties and relationships, not just the ones on which we fix our attention.*

> *The scene we view represents a small subset of the elements of the situation and is in a sense, an artifact of the observation process: we cannot attend to all the elements of a situation, but only to a handful, in the time the scene is accessible to us. This limitation is a limitation in our cognitive capacity, not a limitation inherent in situations under observation.* (Evans, 1985: 02)

The pragmatic study of the speech situations in drama, undertaken here, holds the aforesaid view in its core, planned and developed in five different chapters. The preface introduces the hypotheses, plan and purpose of the study, scope and limitations, selection of dramas and samples for analysis, an overview of the thesis, and some of the major findings.

Hypotheses

1.1 The speech situations in drama do not have any definable static form but rather they are open-ended and marked by the dynamics in their operational mechanism; and this is more so with the speech situations in drama—due to the synchronized play of the social, literary, theatrical, and many a component in the multivalent contexts of drama—than the speech situations in the real life.

1.2 The speech situations in drama have distinctive compositional and operational mechanisms, which require an equally distinctive analytical model for the study.

Justification of the study

The book studies the speech situations in drama in the literary or the print form with a purpose to facilitate the research to evolve an analytical model, which, besides being multi-dimensionally relevant, basically proves its pedagogical relevance and application.

To explore the print form of drama is pedagogically justifiable, as the curriculum of English language and literature at the undergraduate and the postgraduate levels normally contains certain books of drama. Thus, the syllabi mainly prescribe the print form of drama. The pedagogical scope and relevance of the study, hence, begins right at the level of the curriculum design.

The study is a pursuit of the operational mechanism of the speech situations, and don't claim to define any static form of the same since, to define the static form of the speech situations in drama is to isolate them from the overall dramatic decorum, in which they operate holistically.

Hence, the study adopts a holistic perspective and not an isolationistic one.

However, as per the hypothetical claims of this study, though the speech situations don't have any structurally definable identity, they evolve some functionally distinguishable identity in drama. The functional identity can be established on the basis of the components of a speech situation like the ones derived by Leech (1983) and also the ones evolved in the present research.

The aim of exploring the operational mechanism of the situations and not their structure is justifiable also because it falls in line with the pragmatic approach adopted here. The discipline of pragmatics studies the use or the function or the application of language in the contexts, rather than the grammar or the structure or the form of language in isolation.

However, at the same time, the research doesn't totally ignore the grammar of language but, keeping in line with Leech's 'complementarist' (Leech, 1983: X) and 'rhetorical approach' (Leech, 1983: 15) to pragmatics, also studies the use of certain grammatical and semantic aspects in the speech situations in drama.

To brief, the book aims not at defining the structure of communication but pragmatically focuses on the operational dynamism of the communication in drama without ignoring the syntactic and the semantic aspects of the same.

Scope and limitations

The title *Communication in Drama: A Pragmatic Approach* has three basic components viz. pragmatics, communication and drama. Pragmatics is adopted as an approach of the study; communication as the actual topic of the study specified and delimited; and drama as the general area to which the topic of the study belongs. The scope and limitations of the study with regard to these three basic components of the study are discussed below in details.

i) The pragmatic approach

Pragmatics, as an approach to study the communication in drama, investigates the communicational intricacies in the various situations in drama. It studies the situation-specific meanings evolving from the communicational operation and the effects of the language use. Pragmatics offers a set of effective tools to study the communicational operation in drama. According to *Collins Cobuild English Dictionary* (Ed. 1995), '*Pragmatics is the branch of linguistics that deals with the meanings and effects which come from the use of language in particular situations.*' (Sinclair John, ed., 1995: 1289)

The pragmatic approach, precisely, helps pinpoint the communicational intricacies of the various components operating in drama.

ii) Communication in drama as the topic

Communication in drama is the actual topic specified and delimited for the present study. In drama, communication operates in the varied contextual dimensions of society, culture, literature, theatre and so on. These contextual dimensions are discussed as the 'worlds' by Popper (Popper, 1972 in Leech, 1983: 51). The 'worlds' are interrelated; and collectively they form a composite view in drama. As a result, the world view in drama emerges as a very vast area to explore. Hence a delimitation of the present study—specified to communication in drama—is justifiable.

The topic of communication includes a study of the various components of communication viz. addressers and addressees, context and speech acts. Each of these components, in the process of their exploration, undergoes certain classifications clarifying further their scope and limitations.

iii) Drama, the area of study

In the present research drama is the general area of the study to which the specified topic of communication belongs. Drama, as a performing and composite art form, and as a major genre, has a very wide scope, which has been duly delimited as mentioned above. Out of the numerous types of drama, the book focuses on the speech situations in five Indian plays in English, and touches upon some other plays.

Selection of dramas

The book produces a pragmatic analysis of the following plays:

1. *Naga-Mandala* by Girish Karnad (1990)
2. *The Dread Departure* by Satish Alekar (1989)
3. *Ghashiram Kotwal* by Vijay Tendulkar (1986)
4. *Seven Steps around the Fire* by Mahesh Dattani (2000)
5. *Evam Indrajit* by Badal Sircar (1974)

The plays are selected for the study on the basis of their significant contribution to Indian drama; and the samples are selected on the basis of their communicational variations.

All the above playwrights are the major contributors in the development of Indian drama in the post-colonial period. Aparna Dharwadker, the associate professor of theatre and drama and English at the University of Wisconsin-Madison, and the writer of *Theatres of Independence* (Dharwadker, 2005) mentions these playwrights and the plays as the 'major Indian playwrights and plays' during 1950-2004.

Besides enriching the regional drama, these plays have certainly contributed in the emergence of a new 'national canon' (Dharwadker, 2005: 21-53).

An overview

The study views drama from a communicative point of view and analyzes the speech situations in it with a view to the context of linguistics, literature, theatre, society and culture. The wide range of the areas opens up a variety of perspectives, and so requires a 'polyperspectivistic' (Hess-Luttich, 1991: 237) analytical model for the study.

The analytical model is evolved from the following process:

1. Development of a hypothetical model of speech situations based on certain preliminary observations of the communication process in drama
2. Authentication of the hypothetical model by assessing it against the aspects of speech situations described by G.N. Leech (1983)

The analytical model, after its authentication, narrows down the assessment to the three basic components: addressers and addressees, context and speech acts. The assessment of these components brings out many a vital finding, out of which a few are produced below.

Findings

The findings evolved in the study are herewith categorized under two types: the general findings, and the component-specific findings.

General findings

1. Either of the components, viz. the space, the time, the topic and the temporal setup, or all of them together operate/s as the marker/s to distinguish—though not to define and demarcate—one speech situation from the other ones in drama.
2. The operational modes of all the components of a speech situation are found holistically centralized in the message transmission. Hence to assess the 'message' is to assess all the other components centralized in it. Thus the 'message' evolves as the central component.
3. The radio plays, and also the other types of plays, have certain medium-specific strengths and limitations, which influence the author-addresser's communication, and thereby determine both the composition and the transmission of the speech situations.

Component-specific findings

4. The verbal 'sense' gets transformed into the verbal 'force', when certain verbal expressions are used repeatedly and perceived collectively. (From: *Ghashiram Kotwal*, Sample-2)
5. The intensity of the verbal force is language specific, and the interpretation of language is culture-specific, hence the intensity of the verbal force is culture-specific and so does

the intensity of the non-verbal force. (From: *Seven Steps around the Fire*, Sample-1)

6. Indian folklore, by becoming the socio-cultural context of communication in the play, is found to be a connecting factor between the real world and, the literary and the theatrical worlds. (From: *Naga-Mandala*, Sample-1)

7. Various theatrical conventions, being part of the shared knowledge between various addressers and addressees, emerge as the context and operate as the 'contextualization cues' (Kramsch, 1998: 27) for the addressees in the speech situations in drama. (From: *The Dread Departure*, Sample-2)

8. The compositional monotony can arouse the phonetic monotony too. And the act of using the compositional monotony is the author's act that helps the characters' act of executing the phonetic monotony. (From: *Evam Indrajit*, Sample-2)

9. The phatic act of saying something metaphorically and non-verbally is traceable from an act of saying nothing phonetically and verbally. (From: *Seven Steps around the Fire*, Sample-1)

Communication in Drama: A Pragmatic Approach, being an indefinable yet a describable and multi-faceted topic, remains open-ended for many a future possibility of research. Since the topic is open-ended and process-governed, it is justifiably studied here with a process-oriented pragmatic approach, as Leech (1983: 05) says, 'Pragmatics is describable in terms of continuous and indeterminate values.'

To sum up, the book will definitely serve to be a useful reference to all the readers, researchers and scholars interested in this area.

. . . .

CHAPTER-1
INTRODUCTION

1.1 Preliminaries

*C*ommunication in Drama: *A Pragmatic Approach* attempts a systematic explication of the communicational dynamics in the print form of drama, delimited to the operational mechanism of speech situations. The communicational world in drama is neither absolutely fictional, nor absolutely social; hence, it is difficult to outline the same structurally. However, Popper's 'three worlds' (Popper, 1972 in Leech, 1983: 51), and the 'fourth world' (Leech, 1983: 51), extended by Geoffrey Leech, in his *Principles of Pragmatics* (Leech, 1983) certainly facilitate the present research to evolve the operational dynamics of communication in drama, though not the structural frame of it.

Drama, being a composite art form, has literary, theatrical, socio-cultural, and many other dimensions, which operate holistically in it. As a result, the speech situations in drama get processed in the multi-dimensional contexts. For instance, the speech situations in the print form of drama do not operate merely in their literary context, but also in the theatrical, socio-cultural and many other contextual dimensions; and similarly, in a theatrical performance, they don't operate in the theatrical context alone, so on and so forth. Thus, as the operation of the speech situations crosses over the form-specific structure of drama, no demarcation between the speech situations, as absolutely literary or absolutely theatrical is possible. Also, in terms of their 'beginning', 'middle' and 'end' (Butcher, 1951: 274-301), discussed in *Aristotle's Theory of Poetry and Fine Art* (Butcher, 1951), the speech situations in drama do not have any uniform structural frame.

1.1.1 Observation 1

The speech situations in drama are not structurally definable; however they are operationally distinguishable in the communicational world of drama.

On the basis of the operational dynamics, the 'worlds' derived by Popper (1972) and Leech (1983), are also found embedded in the multidimensional communicational world of drama. The three worlds of Popper and the fourth world of Leech are as follows:

> *World 1: the world of physical (including biological) objects, states, etc;*
>
> *World 2: the world of mental (subjective) objects, states, etc;*

World 3: the world of societal objects, states, etc;

World 4: the world of objective facts, existing independently of particular objects, minds, or societies etc.

(Popper, 1972, and Leech, 1983, in Leech, 1983: 52)

The presence of 'World 1' in drama is manifested through the use of physical objects like stage property, and also through the biological presence of performers. The existence of 'World 2' is observed in a concatenation of the mental (subjective) objects and the states of characters, expressed through the 'signaling' (Leech, 1983: 52) or the non-verbal communication in drama. 'World 3' operates through the socio-cultural dimension or the societal objects and the states in drama. The world of objective facts, i.e. 'World 4' in drama, is communicated through the 'linguistic transmission (by text)' (Leech, 1983: 52).

The different worlds in drama open up different perspectives. Hence, a 'polyperspectivistic' (Earnest W.B. Hess-Luttich, 1991 in *Literary Pragmatics*, ed. Sell Roger D, 1991: 237) analysis of the topic is essential here. With a view to this, the study adopts a pragmatic perspective, as pragmatics includes different branches like 'socio-pragmatics, textual pragmatics' (Leech, 1983: 63-70) and 'literary pragmatics' (Mey, 1993: 236-261). However, though these branches can assess the socio-cultural, the textual and the literary aspect of the speech situations, the theatrical dimension of the same may not be assessed properly. Hence, the need for evolving an appropriate model is justifiable here.

1.1.2 Observation 2

In order to assess the multiple dimensions of the speech situations in drama, the study requires a polyperspectivistic analytical model.

On the basis of the observation-1 and the observation-2, the study proposes the following hypotheses:

1. 2 Hypotheses

1.2.1 The speech situations in drama do not have any definable static form but rather they are open-ended and marked by the dynamics in their operational mechanism; and this is more so with the speech situations in drama—due to a synchronized play of the social, literary, theatrical, and many a component in the multivalent contexts in drama—than the speech situations in the real life.

1.2.2 The speech situations in drama have distinctive compositional and operational mechanisms, which require an equally distinctive analytical model for the study.

With the above hypotheses, the research aims at exploring the communicational world of drama in general and the speech situations in particular. The process of communication in drama is viewed here as a communicational performance, according to what, the speech situations are assessed in the context of their communicational performance. In this connection, Austin, in his *How to Do Things with Words* (Austin, 1962) mentions:

Once we realize that what we have to study is not the sentence but the issuing of an utterance in a speech situation, there can hardly be any longer a possibility of not seeing that stating is performing an act. (Austin, 1962: 138)

With reference to the performance-oriented view cited here, the communication in drama is studied below.

1.3 Communication in drama

The communication in drama passes through various channels from a playwright to an audience, depending upon the various mediums of performances like the literary medium, the theatrical medium, the radio medium and so on. Each of these mediums has its own medium-specific communication. Yet, certain dimensions of one medium are found operating in the other mediums also, e.g. the literary dimension operates in the theatrical medium and vice-versa. Hence, in order to encompass the various medium-specific communicational dimensions, operating in each medium, the present study adopts a holistic pragmatic approach. The holistic approach also facilitates the study of various addressers and addressees, e.g. the playwright, the readers, the viewers, the listeners, the actors, the directors and a whole team of the performers in different mediums.

The various performers in the communication process perform their roles at different compositional stages in drama. The stages are distinguished below, with a view to the communicational performance at each stage. Normally, drama, the composite and the performing art, undergoes four compositional stages of communication as follows:

1.3.1 Compositional stages

1) Performance in scripting: the whole writing process of a playwright till the completion of his script.

2) Performance in the print form: the direct communication between the characters in the script; and the indirect communication between the playwright and the audiences (including the readers, the actors, the directors, the technicians and all of those, who read the script of drama).

3) Performance in the non-print form: the role of the performers played face to face as communicators (in a theatrical performance, in a recorded audio-visual performance, in a radio performance, and so on); and the indirect communication, e.g. between the playwright and the various audiences in different mediums.

4) Performance in the reception: the role of the various audiences as the addressees in different mediums.

The above distinction of the compositional stages is an attempt to explicate the intricate communicational performances in drama, in a systematic way. To systematize the study further, certain hypothetical models of communication, based on the above compositional stages, are produced below. Each model explicates the intricate communicational performance of the various communicational 'components' (Mohan K. & Banerji M., 1990: 06) at a particular compositional stage in drama.

At the stage-1 and the stage-4, the type of communication is mainly 'ideational' (Halliday, 1970 & 1973, in Leech, 1983: 56), and partly interpersonal also, i.e. the playwright's transmission at the stage-1 operates personally, where the audiences' end receives it ideationally later at the stage-4; and at the stage-4, the audiences' end operates personally to receive the playwright's ideational transmission, which is composed at the stage-1 earlier. The stage-2 and the stage-3 mainly manifest an 'interpersonal'

(Halliday, 1970 & 1973, in Leech, 1983: 56) type of communication, and also the ideational communication, e.g. between the playwright and the various audiences.

The following figures, fig. 1.3.2.1 to 1.3.2.5, produce the process models of communication at all the four stages, and thereafter the study delimits its scope to the stage-2, i.e. fig.1.3.2.2, wherein the process model of communication in the script of drama is produced. The process models, hereafter, will be referred to as Model-A, Model-B, Model-C, Model-D, and the subtypes of Model-E, as E-1, E-2, E-3, and E-4 respectively. The models are hypothetical and need authentication, which is attempted in the chapter-3 by assessing Model-B (to which the study is delimited) against 'the aspects of speech situations' (Leech, 1983: 13-14) enumerated by Leech.

1.3.2 Hypothetical models

The study proposes the following hypothetical models of communication in drama. Each of these models is produced below in its diagrammatic form. The diagrammatic forms, however, do not describe the structure but the operational mechanism of communication.

1. Model-A: the communicational composition of the script of drama
2. Model-B: the communication in the script of drama

3. Model-C: the communication in the theatrical performance of drama
4. Model-D: the communication in the recorded performance of drama
5. Models E-1 to E-4: The process models of reception in the various communicational mediums of drama

1.3.2.1 Model-A: communicational composition of the script of drama

The communicational performance in scripting

1.3.2.2 Model-B: communication in the script of drama

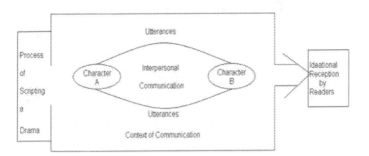

The communicational performance in the print form of drama

1.3.2.3 Model-C: communication in the theatrical performance of drama

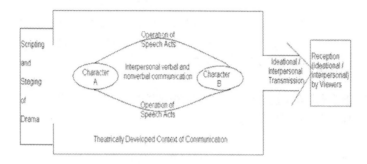

Communication in theatrical performance

1.3.2.4 Model-D: communication in the recorded performance of drama

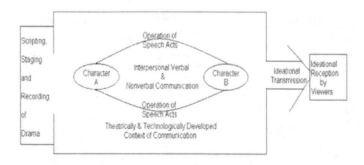

Communication in the recorded performance

1.3.2.5 Models E-1 to E-4: process models of reception

THE PROCESS MODELS OF (READERS', VIEWERS' AND LISTENERS')RECEPTION

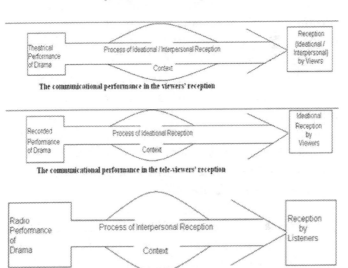

The communicational performance in the readers' reception

The communicational performance in the viewers' reception

The communicational performance in the tele-viewers' reception

The communicational performance in the listeners' reception

The figures: 1.3.2.1 to 1.3.2.5, produce the various process models of communication in drama. Unlike some other models of linear communication—e.g. Saussure's 'speech circuit' (Saussure, 1974, in Chandler, 2002: 176), which is called 'a two-track linear model' (Chandler, 2002: 176)—the models produced here, being process models, are multi-dimensional. The term multi-dimensional here refers to the various communicational dimensions manifested in drama. e.g. the socio-cultural context emerging out of the stage directions in Model-B; the actors' use of body language in Model-C; the technological facilitation in Model-D, and so on (see fig. 1.3.2.1 to 1.3.2.5; and Table-1.3.3).

Precisely, the communication in drama is never a linear kind of verbal communication only, as produced in Saussure's speech circuit. The process of communication in drama is influenced by the various communicational components like the context, the non-verbal means of communication (e.g. the actors' body language), the theatrical and the technological setup, what make this process multi-dimensional. Moreover, the process varies in its composition and operational mechanism from model to model, and so do the speech situations in drama as well.

Table-1.3.3 attempts a distinction between the communication processes in Model-B, Model-C and Model-D. The diagrammatic forms of these models are already produced in fig. 1.3.2.1 to 1.3.2.3.

1.3.3 Model-wise distinction between the communication processes

	Model—B	Model—C	Model—D
Components	Script	Theatrical performance	Recorded performance
Addresser and addressee	Characters in the play	Actor—characters in the play	Actor-characters in the play
Context	Emerges out of stage directions and dialogues	Theatrically developed in the performance	Theatrically developed and technologically facilitated
Message: conversational	Written and mainly verbal	Verbal and non-verbal	Verbal and non-verbal
and narrative	Stage directions about characters' body language, time & place of action etc.	Use of stage property and theatrical elements like music, light effects etc.	Technologically facilitated performance e.g. mixing, dubbing etc.
Transmission channel	Verbal and non-verbal (written form)	Audio-visual; verbal and non-verbal (oral and gestural)	Audio-visual; verbal and non-verbal (oral and gestural)
Reception channel	— '' — '' —	— '' — '' —	— '' — '' —
Communication	Interpersonal	Interpersonal	Interpersonal
Nature of data for assessment	'Dramatic text' (Elam Keir, 1980: 03) in the print form	'Performance text' (Elam Keir, 1980: 03) in the audio-visual non-print form	'Performance text' in the Tele-visual (Hall Stuert,1973) non-print form

On the basis of the distinction attempted in Table-1.3.3, the concept of the speech situations in drama can evolve gradually. However, the three process models in it can evolve three different types of the speech situations in drama. For instance, Model-B, being related to script of drama, can evolve the concept of speech situations in the literary text of drama, whereas, Model-C and Model-D can evolve the speech situations in the theatrical and the recorded performances respectively. Since it is clarifies earlier, the study does not explore every model, but in order to narrow down to a deeper analytical focus, the scope of the present study is delimited to Model-B only. The delimitation of the present research is discussed below.

1.4 Delimitation of the research

Considering the vastness of the communicational area in drama, the study has been delimited to the speech situations in the print form of drama. However, besides and beyond the present delimitation, it is observed that the different communicational mediums overlap each other in the overall process of communication in drama, and the same way the overlapping is manifested, also in the print form of the speech situations in drama.

Hence, with the same holistic approach adopted earlier, the present research explores the process of communication, delimited to the speech situations, in the print form of drama.

1.4.1 Delimitation regarding the plays in translation

The plays selected for the study include some Indian plays in English translation, e.g. Vijay Tendulkar's *Ghashiram Kotwal* (Tendulkar, 1986) translated from Marathi into English by Karve and Zelliot (1999). Such plays are taken as the original works and not as the translated plays. No special perspective like 'pragmatics of translated plays', as found in *The Pragmatics of Translation* (Hickey, 1998); or 'pragmatics of style', as found in *The Pragmatics of Style* (Hickey, 1990) is adopted here. It is for this reason that the areas like the 'translatability', the 'cultural overlap' and the 'cultural diffusion' (Lyons, 1981: 322-329) fall outside the scope of the study. However, besides all the delimitations mentioned above, the study remains open ended for the further research to explore such areas.

After the scope and the delimitation are finalized, a hypothetical model of the speech situations, in the print form of drama, is produced below. The model is derived on the basis of some preliminary observations of the process of communication in Model-B. The following model will be referred to as Model-1 hereafter.

Model-1

Model-1 is developed in two different forms as follows:

The diagrammatic form showing the processing of the speech situations in the script of drama

The components of the speech situation in the script

The two forms of Model-1 are followed by certain preliminary observations of the communicational performance in Model-1.

1.5.1 Diagrammatic form of Model-1

A HYPOTHETICAL MODEL OF SPEECH SITUATIONS IN DRAMA

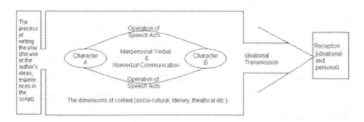

Operational mechanism of the speech situation in the script of drama

1.5.2 Components of Model-1

The components of Model-1 are divided under two parts: A) Compositional components of speech situations; and B) Operational components of speech situations.

1.5.2.1 Compositional components of Model-1

1. **Addressers and addressees**
2. **Context**
3. **Message:**
    i) Conversational message:
       The dialogues in a speech situation

    ii) Narrative message:
       The stage directions in a speech situation

1.5.2.2 Operational components of Model-1

1. **Transmission channel**
2. **Reception channel**
3. **The   type   of   communication**
    (interpersonal, ideational etc.)

1.6 Preliminary observations

The two different forms of Model-1, 1.5.1 and 1.5.2 produced above are developed on the basis of certain preliminary observations. A few of such observations are discussed below.

The diagrammatic form of Model-1 displays certain pragmatic interactions like the operation of speech acts, the verbal and the non-verbal communication, the ideational as well as the interpersonal type of communication etc. More importantly, it also displays a play of the socio-cultural, the literary, and the theatrical contexts in which the entire speech situation is processed.

As far as the socio-cultural context is concerned, an example from the play *The Fire and the Rain* (Karnad, 1998) can be cited here. The utterance, '*The Fire*' in the title needs to be processed in the socio-cultural context, or there are chances of a partial perception of it. The addressees of this utterance would not have the right perception of it, when the utterance is processed in the context of the Indian religious concepts of '*Yadnya*', the sacred fire and '*Homa-havana*', the custom of offering sacred sacrifices to gods.

So far as the literary context is concerned, some previous knowledge of the literary devices like personification—e.g. the personification of 'Flames' as seen in *Naga-Mandala* (Karnad, 1990)—and a previous knowledge of the literary techniques like the use of the stage directions (whereby the use of the characters' non-verbal communication, and the technicians' use of theatrical devices are informed) in drama, operate as the literary context.

The operation of the theatrical context is also thoroughly discussed in the chapters of analysis.

Yet, to mention it briefly, certain speech situations in *Naga-Mandala* (Karnad, 1990) take place in the darkness of night. The darkness, i.e. the time of action is established by the use of light effects, e.g. the meeting of *Rani* and *Naga* at night. A shared knowledge of the use of light effects operates here as the theatrical context, in which this situation is processed. Precisely, it is observed here that Model-1 is processed in the various contextual dimensions, as discussed above.

1.7 Conclusion

The present chapter views the communication in drama, as a communicational performance, by adopting a holistic pragmatic perspective. It also attempts to systematize the study by evolving the various models of communication, operating at the various compositional stages in drama. A very vital outcome of this chapter is Model-1, which facilitates further development of the research.

The next chapter, 'Theoretical Framework', discusses certain significant theoretical concepts related to the present study.

CHAPTER-2

THEORETICAL FRAMEWORK

2.1 Preliminaries

The present chapter prepares a theoretical base for the proposed analysis of speech situations in drama. The concept of speech situations by Leech (1983) is discussed here thoroughly. The chapter also studies the components of speech situations defined by various linguists. In order to prepare a basic theoretical framework, the concepts like Ernest W B Hess-Luttich's (1991) 'model of communication in drama' and Bharat Muni's *Rasa-bhava*[1] theory (see Anandlal, 2004: 308-311) are also referred to. The theoretical discussion in this chapter is aimed at evolving a distinguished analytical model to analyze the speech situations in drama.

So far as the models mentioned above are concerned, they have their own limitations to analyze the speech situations in drama. For instance, Leech's model of 'the aspects of speech situations' (Leech, 1983: 13-15) is a pragmatics-oriented model, which mainly brings to the fore the aspects of the social speech situations and not of the literary ones. Bharat Muni's *Rasa-bhava* theory substantially discusses the various aspects of theatrical communication in spite of which it cannot be applied, as it exists, to the analysis of speech situations in drama, since the dramatics-oriented theory has its own limitations to pinpoint the communicational intricacies pragmatically operating in drama. As compared to the above-mentioned theories of Leech and Bharat Muni, the model of communication in drama, evolved by Ernest W B Hess-Luttich (1991), is much closer to fulfill the requirements of the proposed analysis. The scope of Hess-Luttich model is seen narrowed down to the communicational frame including both the 'dramatic text' (Earnest W B Hess-Luttich in Sell, 1991: 232) as well as the 'performance text' (Earnest W B Hess-Luttich in Sell, 1991: 232). Moreover, this model is evolved on the ground of literary pragmatics. Yet, it cannot be applied, as it exists, to the present study, since it does not focus on the speech situations in particular, but on the overall process of communication in drama. Hence, there is need for a distinguished analytical model suitable for the present study. The following remark of Ernest W B highlights the same.

> *The structure of audio-visual texts like films or theatre performances requires a somewhat more elaborative inventory of analytical instruments than linguists usually provide. In particular, the old*

> *sender-receiver model of communication*
> *is too simple to explain the communicative*
> *relationship between the participants of*
> *dialogues presented to audiences in theatre*
> *plays.* (Ernest W B: 1991 in Sell, 1991: 232)

So, to evolve a suitable analytical model, it is essential to discuss the various views on the concept of speech situations. Leech, in his *Principles of Pragmatics* (Leech, 1983), has elaborated his concept of speech situations. The various aspects of his concept are as follows:

2.2 Leech's concept of speech situations

Leech, while working on the principles of pragmatics, derives various aspects of speech situations. So, it is obvious that his model has no direct concern with drama as such. As far as drama is concerned, the communication in general and the speech situations in particular operate very distinctively in drama than the same operate in the social scenario. Obviously, the notion like pragmatics of communication in drama is bound to be equally distinctive. Hence, although Leech's model lays some authentic grounding for the proposed analysis, further exploration for a suitable model is essential. Prior to this, Leech's model needs be discussed. According to Leech, there are mainly the following aspects of speech situations:

1. Addressers or addressees
2. Context of an utterance

3. Goal(s) of an utterance
4. Utterance as a form of act or activity : a speech act
5. Utterance as a product of a verbal act

In addition to the above mentioned aspects, Leech inclines to accommodate some more aspects like 'the time' and 'the place' of an utterance in his concept. In this respect, Leech mentions:

> *From the above-mentioned elements of (i) addresser and addressee, (ii) context, (iii) goals, (iv) illocutionary act and (v) utterance, we can compose a notion of a SPEECH SITUATION, comprising all these elements, and perhaps other elements as well, such as the time and the place of the utterance.* (Leech, 1983: 15)

Thus the components like the time and the place of an utterance also can be some more aspects of the speech situations. In this sense, Leech keeps his model open-ended.

2.3 Leech's model and the views of others

In the process of evolving the analytical model, at this stage, it is essential to discuss the different aspects of speech situations derived by Leech against the views on the same by others. An aspect-by-aspect theoretical discussion is worked out here.

2.3.1 Addressers—addressees

According to Leech—who holds *a* 'complementarist view of pragmatics within an overall programme for studying language as a communication system', that is, 'studying the use of a language as distinct form, but complementary to, the language itself seen as a formal system' (Leech, 1983: X)— conceptually, the 'addressers' means both 'a speaker' and 'a writer', whereas, the 'addressees' means 'a hearer' or 'a receiver' or 'a reader' (Leech, 1983: 13). Austin (1962), Searle (1969), and some others use the terms 'speaker ('s') and hearer ('h')' for the addresser and the addressee respectively. Since Austin's and Searle's terms are related more to the oral communication than to the written dialogic communication, as it is in drama, comparatively, Leech's complementary approach is found more applicable to the speech situations in drama. Even David Evans's (1985) approach supports Leech's complementarist view. Evans elaborates on both the oral and the written communication. He differentiates between the two as follows:

> *Not only are the tasks different (in one case we must attend to the addressee and make our words conform to his needs at the moment; in the other we must imagine and interpret both roles of speaker and addressee, simultaneously) but the words we use, the rules we observe, are different too.*

Regarding the difference in the effect of oral and written expression, Evans further mentions:

> *Expressing an idea on a single occasion to a particular individual involves different problems than expressing the same idea to an unknown addressee (potentially, anyone), who may encounter the written expression of our thoughts on any occasion.* (Evans, 1985: 08)

As far as the communication in drama is concerned, Evans's approach very well matches with that of Leech's complementary approach, and thus, Leech's conception of the addresser-addressee proves to be suitable in the present study. Goffman (1974) derives the different entities invoked by a speaker in his talk as follows:

i) *An animator who speaks the words*
ii) *An author, who prepares the word*
iii) *A principal, who is responsible for the word*
iv) *A figure animated by the speaker* (Goffman in Patil, 2004: 10)

Goffman's view is very close to the addressers and addressees operating in drama. Gordon Craig's (1911) view on the 'spoken word'[2] also resembles Goffman's view referred to above.

2.3.2 Context of an utterance

The conception of context should be described as the widest of all the aspects of speech situations. The vast area of context has been explored from different perspectives, e.g. as 'context of situation', 'context of culture' etc. (Halliday and Hasan, 1989; Kramsch Claire, 1998; and others). Malinowski (1935) correlates the study of context with the activities performed in the actual situation. According to Malinowski:

> *It is very profitable in linguistics to widen the concept of context so that it embraces not only spoken words but facial expression, gesture, bodily activities, the whole group of people present during an exchange of utterances and the part of the environment on which these people are engaged.* (Malinowski, 1935: 22)

Leech (1983) views the present conception as the 'context of an utterance' (Leech, 1983: 13). What Leech, here, means by context is 'any background knowledge assumed to be shared by **s** and **h,** and which contributes to **h's** interpretation of what **s** means by a given utterance' (Leech, 1983: 13). At the same time, Leech mentions one of the others' 'understandings' of context i.e. the context understood as 'the 'relevant' aspects of the physical or social setting of an utterance' (Leech, 1983: 13).

Although, on the vast map of context, Leech narrows down to the context of an utterance i.e. the mutually shared background knowledge by 's' and 'h', in fact, such a shared context too is so vast as to accommodate a lot of emotional, social, historical, cultural, mythical, religious, political and the like of the elements in it. A sample produced below shows certain evidences of the same. It is collected from Girish Karnad's play *The Fire and the Rain* (Karnad, 1998) wherein a pair of lovers belonging to different communities is seen sorting out the worries in the settlement of their marriage, especially the worries of the lover in courting his would be wife. Certain social customs, cultural and religious discrepancies between their communities are the major hurdles they have to cross over. The same hurdles they know about are the mutually shared context between the interlocutors here. This context, dense with the social, the cultural and the religious customs, surges out through the utterance, 'the elders' (Karnad, 1998: 05). The utterance brings out the density of the context in the following excerpt.

*NITTILAI: Oh! Don't go on about it! I told you! There's nothing to worry about. **The elders** (emphasized by the researcher) will gather under the big banyan tree and ask a few questions. You answer them . . . .*

*ARVASU: I couldn't sleep a wink last night. Woke up in a cold sweat every time I thought of **your elders** (emphasized by the researcher) . . . .*

(Karnad, 1998: 05)

'The elders' from the above excerpt operates as a context-marker. It does not mean only the elders i.e. the elderly people from Nittilai's Hunter community. Its situational implicature is far more than that. It voices the social customs, and the cultural, and the religious disparity between the communities of Nittilai and Arvasu, respectively Hunter and Brahmin. It also does voice the worries of the two, because the same stand as the hurdle in the settlement of their marriage. From the excerpt, it is found that the utterance 'the elders' has certain social, cultural, and religious background knowledge, which can be assumed to be shared by the 's' (Nittilai) and the 'h' (Arvasu), and which contributes to the 'h's' interpretation of what the 's' means by the given utterance. Thus, Leech's conception of 'the context of an utterance' (Leech, 1983: 13) operates very well here. However, the real objective behind this discussion is to show how the social, the cultural, the religious, and the like of elements have their play in the *context of an utterance*. The utterance 'the elders' voices the interlocutors' keen concern about and the worries due to the elders; and evidently it can be seen that the concern and the worries emerge out of certain social, cultural, and religious elements in the background. This becomes evident in the following part of the same speech situation produced below:

NITTILAI: You are a fuss-pot. You've known them for years. And after all, every young man about to get married goes through it. Just declare—

ARVASU: Yes, I know. I know: Just stand there and say: 'I want to take her as my wife. I am potent. I can satisfy all her needs . . . .

NITTILAI: (Shyly.) Yes, more or less, that!

ARVASU: And in public!

NITTILAI: Of course. What's the point of saying it to yourself? (Laughs.) Don't worry. It's nothing . . . .

ARVASU: Nothing, yes. For the young men of your tribe! But I am a Brahmin. To say all that in plain, loud words to a smirking, nudging, surging multitude. No hymns to drown out one's voice. No smoke to hide behind. It's dreadful. I hope there won't be too many people there

(Karnad, 1998: 05)

The speech situation explicitly clarifies that the context of the utterance 'the elders' is social, cultural, as well as religious in nature. The following illustration throws light on the same.

2.3.2.1 Contextual elements of the utterance

The contextual elements of the utterance 'the elders' are produced below:

i) **Social element:** the social custom of courting a girl in the hunter's tribe.

ii) **Cultural element:** the cultural disparity between the two communities i.e. the act of proposing a girl publicly and too openly in the Hunters' community, as considered against the same act practiced among the Brahmins in the cultural garb of the hymns and the sacred fire.

iii) **Religious element:** the religious disparity between the two communities i.e. the religious rites of chanting the hymns and having the sacred fire at the time of courting and marrying a girl, as observed among the Brahmins and the same not observed among the Hunters.

Besides being social, cultural, religious, and the like, the context of an utterance in drama can bring out yet more dimensions in its operation. The various dimensions of the context of utterances in drama are thoroughly explored in the chapters of analysis.

2.3.3 Goal(s) of an utterance

Leech, while stating the third aspect of his concept i.e. 'the goal(s) of an utterance' (Leech, 1983: 13), differentiates the same from a controversial term, 'the intended meaning' (Leech, 1983: 13).

Leech argues:

> *I shall often find it useful to talk of a goal or function of an utterance, in*

preference to talking about its intended meaning, or s's intention in uttering it. The term goal is more neutral than intention, because it does not commit its user to dealing with conscious volition or motivation, but can be used generally of goal-oriented activities. The term intention can be misleading on this score. (Leech, 1983: 13)

The speaker's intention in communication has been a problem area. Hence, it is discussed below.

2.3.3.1 Speaker's intention in communication

The speaker's intention in communication has been an important as well as a controversial point in the study of pragmatics. Although, Leech calls it to be misleading on this score, the others have their own different perspectives about it. For instance, the classical code model of communication as referred to in *The Handbook of Pragmatics* (Sperber and Wilson, 2004: 607), Grice's (1975) founded inferential model of communication and Sperber and Wilson's (2004) relevance theory opine differently on this point. In *The Handbook of Pragmatics* (Laurence R. Horn and Gregory Ward Ed., 2004: 607-632), Sperber and Wilson, while surveying the same point, mention:

According to the code model, a communicator encodes her intended

> *message into a signal, which is decoded*
> *by the audience using an identical copy*
> *of the code.* (Sperber and Wilson in *The*
> *Handbook of Pragmatics*, 2004: 607)

On the one hand, when the classical code model takes 'the speaker's intention' for granted, on the other hand even the inferential model of Grice—who according to Sperber and Wilson (2004), laid the foundations for an inferential model of communication as an alternative to the classical code model—elaborates on the play of the speaker's intention in communication. Grice, in this connection, says, 'an essential feature of most human communication is the expression and recognition of intentions' (Grice in Retrospective Epilogue, 1989: Essays 1-7, 14, 18). According to the inferential model, 'a communicator provides evidence of her intention to convey a certain meaning, which is inferred by the audience on the basis of the evidence provided' (see Grice: 1961, 1967, 1975, and 1989). Sperber and Wilson's relevance theory also shares some of Gricean claims. For instance, they say:

> *Relevance theory may be seen as an*
> *attempt to work out in details one of*
> *Grice's central claims: that an essential*
> *feature of most human communication*
> *is the expression and recognition of*
> *intentions.* (Sperber and Wilson in *The*
> *Handbook of Pragmatics*, 2004: 607)

Sperber and Wilson, besides emphasizing the Gricean claim, produce the central claim of their own theory, which, in a way, connects 'the expression and the recognition of intention' by means of the precise and predictable relevance raised by an utterance. According to Wilson and Sperber:

> *The central claim of relevance theory is that the expectations of relevance raised by an utterance are precise and predictable enough to guide the hearer toward the speaker's meaning. The aim is to explain in cognitively realistic terms what these expectations amount to, and how they might contribute to an empirically plausible account of comprehension.* (Wilson and Sperber in *The Handbook of Pragmatics*, 2004: 607-608)

'The relevance raised by an utterance' emerges as the central and connecting element between the speaker's intention and the hearer's inference of an utterance. In this connection, Leech's conception, 'the goal(s) of an utterance' (Leech, 1983: 13), is much similar to the central concern of the relevance theory, as both the conceptions think along the connecting element between the speaker's intention and the hearer's inference of an utterance. Precisely, the central concern of Wilson and Sperber as well as Leech, lies in the use of language, rather than in the users of language. Wilson and Sperber centrally focus on the relevance raised by an utterance, whereas Leech focuses on the goal-oriented activities. Leech justifies the same as follows:

> *The term goal is more neutral than intention, because it does not commit its user to dealing with conscious volition or motivation, but can be used generally of goal-oriented activities. The term intention can be misleading on this score.* (Leech, 1983: 13)

Leech further elaborates his notion of the goal and the goal-oriented activities in his model of the 'means-ends analysis' (Leech, 1983: 40) as follows:

> *The term 'goal' is slightly restrictive, and the term 'intention' even more so, in suggesting a degree of conscious or deliberate planning of discourse which the model does not necessarily imply . . . . In short the term goal is used in the neutral Artificial Intelligence sense of 'a state which regulates the behaviour of the individual' in such a way as to facilitate a given outcome.* (Leech, 1983: 40)

Leech is keenly concerned with the behaviour of individuals and the similar kinds of goal-oriented activities that facilitate a certain outcome in the use of language. To Leech, the means used to reach the ends i.e. the activity operating as the connecting element between the speaker's expression and the hearer's recognition of intention is the central concern, which resembles Wilson and Sperber's central concern of the relevance raised by an utterance.

As far as drama is concerned, the central concern with regard to the goal(s) of an utterance has to be again the use of language rather than the users of language, since in drama not the actual addresser-addressees i.e. the playwright and the audience directly converse but the characters operate as the interlocutors. On this ground, when the actual users of language in drama are not clearly definable, the study of the goal(s) of an utterance will be more logical and authentic by studying the use of language rather than the users of language. Thus, in the study of the speech situations in drama, the goal(s) of an utterance should be studied by assessing the goal-oriented activities, as Leech says and / or by assessing the relevance raised by an utterance, as Wilson and Sperber say.

2.4 The utterance as a form of act or activity: a speech act

In pragmatics, the speech is thought to be action and the utterances acts. 'The speech-act theory' (Austin: 1962 and Searle: 1969) undertakes the study of such acts performed by the utterances. Austin (1962), Searle (1969), Leech (1983), and some others too share the similar view regarding this aspect of the speech situations. According to Leech:

> *Grammar deals with abstract static entities such as sentences (in syntax and propositions (in semantics), pragmatics deals with verbal acts or performances which take place in particular situations, in time. In this respect pragmatics deals with language at a more concrete level than grammar.* (Leech, 1983: 14)

Leech's comparison of pragmatics with grammar is desirable here, especially to highlight the concrete level of pragmatics as compared to the abstract level of grammar. The concrete level of pragmatics obviously refers to the action or 'the verbal acts performed in saying something' i.e. the 'illocutionary act' (Austin, 1962: 120). In Leech's *Principles of Pragmatics* (Leech, 1983), the 'verbal acts or performances taking place in particular situations, in time' (Leech, 1983: 15) are nothing else but Leech's conception of the illocutionary act evolved on analyzing and revising Austin's conception of illocutionary act (see 'Speech-act verbs in English', Leech, 1983: 198-228). According to Austin, an illocutionary act is 'Performing an act **in** saying something.' (Austin, 1962: 120)

The acts performed in saying something are obviously some 'linguistic behaviour' (Leech, 1983:

201) and in Austin's concept the status of the same, Leech finds out, is singular one, whereas, according to Leech, 'Linguistic behaviour is made up of complexes of activity, rather than of single events . . . . . . as in the means-ends model.' (Leech, 1983: 201)

Thus, the linguistic behavior—that includes the complexes of activity in saying something (i.e. the illocutionary act)—precisely clarifies the operating mode of the illocutionary act, i.e. 'the utterance as a form of act or activity: a speech act' (Leech, 1983: 14), the fourth aspect of Leech's concept of speech situations.

In drama, there is a lot of scope to study such complexes of activity in saying something. The utterances in drama can certainly be studied from the viewpoint of the complexes of activity performed by the users of language i.e. by the characters in drama in performing the verbal acts.

2.5 The utterance as a product of a verbal act

Leech views utterance mainly in two distinctive forms: the utterance as a form of act or activity: a speech act; and 'the utterance as a product of a verbal act' (Leech, 1983: 14). According to Leech, the term utterance refers to 'the product of a verbal act, rather than to the verbal act itself' (Leech, 1983: 14). It is one of the very important aspects of Leech's concept of speech situations. Leech describes the utterance as a product of a verbal act, wherein he states 'When we try to work out the meaning of an utterance . . . thus the meaning of an utterance, in this sense, can be called its illocutionary force.' (Leech, 1983: 14, 15)

Leech describes the utterance as the illocutionary force i.e. as the product of a verbal act, since the utterance, in the form of the illocutionary force, operates at the **product stage,** out of the various stages, of a verbal act. Leech, thus, specifies the operating scope of the utterance here, especially to the product stage and calls utterance a product, the **illocutionary force.** Regarding the meaning of the illocutionary force and especially to distinguish it from the illocutionary act (the third aspect of Leech's concept) Leech states, 'Illocutionary force is the communicative plan or design behind s's remark . . . and the illocutionary act is the fulfillment of that communicative goal'. (Leech, 1983: 200)

If the utterance is called an illocutionary force, and if the illocutionary force is the communicative plan, then **the operating scope of the utterance can be seen stretched back from the earlier discussed product stage to the plan stage of a verbal act.** In addition to this, Leech clearly describes even the fourth aspect of his concept, the illocutionary act as 'the utterance as a form of act or activity: a speech act' (Leech, 1983: 14). Here, the operating scope of the utterance—which thus functions through the act or activities—can also be seen spread between even the plan stage and the product stage of the verbal act. That means, the operating scope of the utterance, the last aspect of Leech's concept, encompasses the area from the communicative plan stage in s's mind, through the middle stage, the act / activity, to the product stage of a verbal act.

Precisely, according to Leech's concept of speech situations, the utterance is found operating at three different stages:

1) The (communicative) plan;
2) The act / activity; and
3) The product.

However, Leech here mainly comments on the product stage of utterance only, as the other stages of the utterance fall outside the scope of the present point.

Besides the above-discussed five aspects of speech situations, Leech hints at the possibility of some more aspects like the time and place of the utterance. Such possibilities are discussed below.

2.6. The other aspects of speech situations

After enumerating the five aspects of speech situations as above, Leech mentions:

> *From the above-mentioned elements of*
> *(i) addresser and addressee, (ii) context,*
> *(iii) goals, (iv) illocutionary act, and (v)*

> *utterance, we can compose a notion of a SPEECH SITUATION, comprising all these elements, and perhaps other elements as well, such as the time and the place of the utterance. Pragmatics is distinguished from semantics in being concerned with meaning in relation to a speech situation.* (Leech, 1983: 15)

As the time, the place, and such aspects of the utterance can contribute in comprising a speech situation, the possibilities of new aspects are greater in dramatic speech situations. For instance, the time of any reported action in drama can become an additional aspect of a speech situation in that play. This can be supported by an example mentioned by Leech. The example is cited below:

	s	IA (t)	h	U
[1] Direct speech (action):	"I	order	you	to stand up."
[2] Reported speech (action):	He	ordered	them	to stand up.

According to Leech: *Both* [1] *and* [2] *name a speech situation, of which the components are:*

s = speaker	h = addressee
IA = illocutionary act	U = utterance
t = time of speech act.	(Leech, 1983: 181)

Here, the time of speech act emerges as an additional aspect of the speech situations. In the same way, even the place of action can operate as an additional aspect.

While the aspects of speech situations are under discussion, some closely related concepts like speech events and speech acts are also significant in the present theoretical discussion.

2.7 Speech situations, speech events, and speech acts

Hymes (1972) makes a hierarchical distinction between the three closely interrelated concepts, as entitled above. Hymes's hierarchy showing the place of each of these units is accepted widely. According to Hymes, the three units make a 'nested hierarchy' (Hymes, 1972: 58), wherein the speech acts are the part of the speech events which are, in turn, the part of the speech situations.

2.7.1 Speech situations

Hymes describes speech situations as 'situations associated with (or marked by the absence of) speech' (Hymes, 1972: 58). In this sense, the speech situations may not be purely communicative always, but they may comprise both the communicative as well as the other kinds of events. In this regard, Hymes's conception, the 'speech situations are not themselves subject to the rules of speaking, but can be referred to by the rules of speaking as context' (Hymes, 1972: 58), seems to be very logical.

2.7.2 Speech events

Regarding the speech events, on the other hand, Hymes mentions, 'the speech events are both communicative and governed by rules for the use of speech' (Hymes, 1972: 58). He further says, 'a speech event takes place within a speech situation and is composed of one or more speech acts' (Hymes, 1972: 58). To illustrate the same he mentions an example of a joke in the conversation at a party, wherein the joke might be a speech act, which is part of the conversation i.e. a speech event, which takes place at the party i.e. a speech situation. According to Hymes, 'it is also possible for a speech act to be, in itself, the entire speech event, which might be the only event in a speech situation.' (Hymes, 1972: 58-59) Thus a single speech act can be, sometimes, an entire speech situation in itself.

2.7.2.1 Speech events as the activity types

Levinson (1979) prefers the term, activity type, to the term, speech event, and defines it as 'any culturally recognized activity, whether or not that activity is co-extensive with a period of speech or indeed whether any talk takes place in it at all' (Levinson, 1979, in Grundy, 2000: 170). According to Grundy, 'to understand properly the structure of an activity type or speech event is to account for the roles of the speech acts that make it up' (Grundy, 2000: 170). From the conceptions of Levinson and Grundy, the dimensions like time, occasion, culture and speech act emerge as the constituents of a speech event. Although Levinson uses the term, the activity type, the term used for the same in the thesis is the speech event.

2.7.3 Speech acts

The speech act, as seen above, emerges as 'the minimal term of the set' (Hymes, 1972: 56). However, according to Hymes, 'A speech act is the simplest and, at the same time, the most troublesome unit.' (Hymes, 1972: 56)

Being the minimal term of the set it is the simplest unit, and it becomes the troublesome unit, especially when a single speech act gets the status of an entire speech situation, as illustrated above. In such a case, according to Hymes, the speech act gets its status from the social context as well as the grammatical form and intonation. Hymes mentions:

> *The level of speech acts mediates immediately between the usual levels of grammar and the rest of a speech event or speech situation in that it implicates both linguistic form and social norms.* (Hymes, 1972: 57)

As far as the analysis of the speech acts goes, the above mentioned problem evolves different levels for the analysis of the speech acts e.g. the syntactic level, the phonological level, the level of the socio-cultural context etc. Besides the analytical base of these levels, the study of the speech acts also needs a review of the types and subtypes of the speech acts, as emerged from the works of Austin (1962), Searle (1969) and the others.

2.8 The types and subtypes of speech acts

The types and sub-types of the speech acts can best be studied by studying the different perspectives on the same, e.g. the Austinian perspective, the Searlean perspective, the Leechian perspective etc. A short review of the speech-act theory proposed by Austin (1962), and further developed by Searle (1969); and the views of Leech (1983) on the same, besides the views of some others, can certainly shape up the proposed analytical model required for the assessment of the speech acts, 'the basic or minimal units of linguistic communication' (Searle, 1969: 16).

2.9 Austinian perspective on speech acts

The William James Lectures delivered by Austin (1955) at the Harvard University in 1955, and thereafter published in the form of his *How to Do Things with Words* (Austin, 1962), proposed Austin's theory of the speech acts. The theory was developed further by Searle (1969). In his speech-act theory, Austin initially proposed his doctrine of the distinction of the utterances as the 'constatives' and the 'performatives' (Austin, 1962:

47). These two types, roughly speaking, stand for 'saying' and 'doing' respectively. While reviewing the types of the speech acts, it is essential to touch upon the said distinction also, since, the significance of the 'constative-performative distinction in the theory of speech acts is as the special theory is to the general theory' (Austin, 1962: 147). According to Austin, 'This is one way in which we might justify the 'performative-constative' distinction—the distinction between doing and saying.' (Austin, 1962: 47)

Further, in connection with the said distinction, Austin mentions:

(a) *With the constative utterance, we abstract from the illocutionary (let alone the perlocutionary) aspects of the speech act, and we concentrate on the locutionary: . . . . an oversimplified notion of correspondence with the facts.*

(b) *With the performative utterance, we attend as much as possible to the illocutionary force of the utterance, and abstract from the dimension of correspondence with facts.* (Austin, 1962: 144-145)

Though, thus, Austin initiates with a focus on the distinction between utterances, his motive, basically, remains to propose the speech-act theory. To clarify it he mentions:

> *The doctrine of the performative /
> constative distinction stands to the
> doctrine of locutionary and illocutionary
> acts in the total speech act as the
> special theory to the general theory.*
> (Austin, 1962: 147)

In his proposition of the speech-act theory, Austin discusses mainly three types of speech acts:

i) Locutionary speech act (inclusive of the Phonetic, the Phatic, and the Rhetic acts)
ii) Illocutionary speech act
iii) Perlocutionary speech act

Austin, hereby, also distinguishes some vital aspects of these acts, whereby the distinction of each act from the other is facilitated:

> *Thus we distinguished the locutionary
> act (and within it the the phonetic, the
> phatic, and the rhetic acts) which has a
> meaning; the illocutionary act which has
> a certain force in saying something; the
> perlocutionary act which is the achieving
> of certain effects by saying something.*
> (Austin, 1962: 120)

2.9.1 Locutionary speech act

Prior to making his final classification of the speech acts, with regard to the element of 'meaning' in the locutionary act, Austin mentions that a 'locutionary act is roughly equivalent to uttering a certain sentence with a certain sense and reference, which again is roughly equivalent to 'meaning' in the traditional sense'. (Austin, 1962: 108) Thus, the meaning element, according to Austin, is inclusive of a certain sense and reference. Besides these details of the locutionary act, it is also important to note here that the sense and reference of an utterance can come out through the phonetic or the phatic or the rhetic acts, since these acts, according to Austin's above-mentioned proposition, make a locutionary act. It is also important here to distinguish between the phonetic, the rhetic and the phatic acts. Leech, in his *Principles of Pragmatics* (Leech, 1983), interprets the phonetic act. According to Leech, Austin uses 'the term phonetic act for the actual physical execution of the utterance; and Austin uses the terms the rhetic and the phatic acts as corresponding to the semantic and syntactic levels of coding respectively' (Leech, 1983: 200). While Leech interprets the subtypes of the locutionary act precisely, an explanation on these subtypes by Austin himself clears the same elaborately. What Austin mentions and Leech doesn't mention (perhaps because Leech's main focal point was not the locutionary act but the principles of pragmatics) is the element of lexis or the 'vocabulary' element from the phatic act—Austin says, 'In the definition of the phatic act two things were lumped together: vocabulary and grammar' (Austin: 1962: 96)—and the 'more-or-less definite sense and reference' (Austin, 1962: 95) from the rhetic act. Thus, there are some vital aspects of distinction also between the subtypes of the locutionary act. Austin mentions:

> *The phonetic act is merely the act of uttering certain noises. The phatic act is the uttering of certain vocables or words, i.e. noises of certain types, belonging to and as belonging to, a certain vocabulary, conforming to and as conforming to a certain grammar. The rhetic act is the performance of an act of using those vocables with a certain more-or-less definite sense and reference.* (Austin, 1962: 95)

The distinction of the phonetic act from the rest seems easier to comprehend. The phatic and the rhetic acts are further distinguished by Austin. According to Austin, 'He said "The cat is on the mat"' (Austin, 1962: 95), reports a phatic act, whereas 'He said that the cat was on the mat' (Austin, 1962: 95) reports a rhetic act.

While interpreting the vital aspects of distinction between the sub-types of locutionary act, and while clarifying the distinction between the main types of the speech acts, it should also be noted here that these speech acts are linked with each other and that the said distinction is discussed here for the convenience of presentation, especially to facilitate a well-knit analysis of the various speech acts, which are in a 'nested hierarchy' (Hymes, 1972:

56-59) or 'in a chain of events' (Leech, 1983: 200). According to Leech:

> *The main point is that the different kinds of speech act can be interpreted as comprising a hierarchy of instrumentality, one act forming a link in chain of events which constitute another act, further up the hierarchy.* (Leech, 1983: 200)

After distinguishing the place of the locutionary act, along with its intricate details, in the nested hierarchy or in the chain of events, the present discussion concludes with Austin's distinction of this act on the basis of the element of performance as follows::

> LOCUTION: *s* says to *h* that *X*.
> (*X* being certain words spoken with a *certain sense and reference*) (Austin, 1962 as referred to in Leech, 1983: 199)

Thus, finally, Austin defines the locutionary act as 'performing an act of saying something'. (Austin, 1962: 94) In chain with the locutionary act, the discussion continues with the following perspective on the illocutionary act.

2.9.2 Illocutionary speech act

According to Austin, the illocutionary speech act is 'performing an act in saying something', and also the act, which has 'a certain force in saying something' (Austin, 1962: 120). Prior to reaching this precision, Austin discusses the notion of the illocutionary act thoroughly. Austin elaborates:

> *To determine what illocutionary act is performed we must determine in what way we are using the locution: asking or answering a question, giving some information or an assurance or a warning, announcing a verdict or an intention, pronouncing a sentence, making an appointment or an appeal or a criticism, making an identification or giving a description, and the numerous like. (I am not suggesting that this is a clearly defined class by any means.)*
> (Austin, 1962: 98-99)

By referring to the above-mentioned and other numerous ways of using the locution, Austin brings out the notion of the illocutionary force in the illocutionary act. The illocutionary force emerges as a decisive factor in determining any utterance to be an advice or a mere suggestion or an order, and any other utterance to be a strictly promise or an announcement of only a vague intention. The different debatable functions of language, like the above-mentioned ones, become determinable by determining the illocutionary force with which they are used. Austin, in this connection, mentions 'I shall refer to the doctrine of the different types of function of language in question as the doctrine of 'illocutionary forces'.' (Austin, 1962: 99)

It seems quite logical here that the illocutionary force determines what specific function of the language is under operation. However, it arouses some important questions:

1. How to determine the type of illocutionary force e.g., as the force of an order and not of an advice or a mere suggestion?
2. How to differentiate between one type of force and the other similar force e.g. the force of a promise from that of an announcement of only a vague intention?

These questions will certainly matter in the actual analysis of the speech situations in drama in the forthcoming chapters. At the present stage, although, roughly it seems that it is the speaker's intention that should determine the type of illocutionary force, and also should differentiate between the illocutionary forces similar to each other, there must be some other factors also that shape up the illocutionary force. Some of such factors, related to the use of language, rather than to the users of language, can be traced from the following comment by Austin. Austin, with respect to this, mentions:

> *For some years we have been realizing*
> *more and more clearly that the occasion*
> *of an utterance matters seriously, and*

> *that the words used are to some extent*
> *to be 'explained' by the context in which*
> *they are designed to be or have actually*
> *been spoken in a linguistic interchange.*
> (Austin, 1962: 100)

Thus, the occasion of an utterance, the context, the actual linguistic interchange, so on and so forth, can operate as the factors determining the nature of the illocutionary force. This point, though hints at some factors, needs some detailed investigation, which can be carried out in the forthcoming chapters of analysis.

Thus, by placing the conception of the illocutionary force at its center, Austin concludes his concept of the illocutionary speech act as: performing an act, which has a certain force in saying something. To clarify the same technically, Austin puts it in the following formula.

'In saying x I was doing y' or 'I did y'. (Austin, 1962: 121)

Here x is the locution, while y is the illocution e.g. 'In saying I would shoot him I was threatening him'.

In brief, Austin's concept of the illocutionary act centers on the conception of the illocutionary force, with reference to which, the verbal illocutionary forces and the non-verbal illocutionary forces are studied under the illocutionary speech act in the chapters of analysis.

2.9.3 Perlocutionary speech act

The perlocutionary act, according to Austin, is performing an act for the 'achieving of certain effects by saying something' (Austin, 1962: 120). Austin brings out his conception of the perlocutionary act by comparing the same with the other two acts viz. the locutionary act and the illocutionary act. He puts the distinction between them as follows:

> *Act (A) or Locution*
> *e.g. He said to me, 'You can't do that'.*
>
> *Act (B) or Illocution*
> *e.g. He protested against my doing it.*
>
> *Act (C.a) or Perlocution*
> *e.g. He pulled me up, checked me.*
>
> *Act (C.b)*
> *e.g. He stopped me, he brought me to my senses, &c.*
> *He annoyed me.* (Austin, 1962: 102)

Austin uses these examples to bring out the conceptual distinction between the three acts, and further explores some intricate aspects of the perlocutionary act. The intricacy in his conception arises out of the 'consequence' or the 'effect' element, which gives rise to **a dichotomy between the speaker-intended effects and the speaker-unintended effects**. Austin himself describes this problem as, 'the usual troubles and reservations about attempt as distinct from achievement, being intentional as distinct from being unintentional and the like' (Austin, 1962: 109). Austin traces the problem and segregates the ways in which the effects can occur. He segregates it as:

> *The distinction between producing effects or consequences which are intended or unintended; and (i) when the speaker intends to produce an effect it may nevertheless not occur, and (ii) when he does not intend to produce it or intends not to produce it, it may nevertheless occur.* (Austin, 1962: 105)

After discussing the aforesaid distinction, Austin clarifies another important aspect of the perlocutionary act. It is about the stretch of the perlocutionary act. Austin says, 'there is no restriction to the minimum physical act at all that we can import an indefinitely long stretch of what might also be called the 'consequences'' (Austin, 1962: 106). He clarifies his notion of the indefinite stretch of the consequence with the following example.

> *If asked 'what did he do?', we may reply either 'He shot the donkey' or 'He fired a gun' or 'He pulled the trigger' or 'He moved his trigger finger', and all may be correct.*(Austin, 1962: 107)

While the notions: the minimum physical act and the indefinite stretch of perlocution, find some place in the conception of the perlocutionary act, Austin, in sequence with the notion of the physical act, opens up yet another important characteristic, wherein the perlocution is achieved by '**non-locutionary means**', and which is very much relevant in the study of speech situations in drama. According to Austin:

> *It is characteristic of perlocutionary acts that the response achieved, or the sequel, can be achieved additionally or entirely by non-locutionary means: thus intimidation may be achieved by waving a stick or pointing a gun. Even in the cases of convincing, persuading, getting to obey and getting to believe, we may achieve the response non-verbally.*
> (Austin, 1962: 117-118)

The non-locutionary means obviously are the non-verbal means of communication that are studied under the different branches like 'Kinesics' (Birdwhistell, 1952), 'Paralanguage' (Welmers, 1954) and 'Proxemics' (Hall Edward, 1966). Mary Key in her *Paralanguage and Kinesics* (Key Mary, 1975) mentions the significance of the 'temporal aspects' (Key Mary, 1975: 128) in the non-verbal communication. According to Key, 'Temporal aspects affect the communication behaviour.' (Key Mary, 1975: 128)

The speech situations in drama show the play of such non-verbal means, operating effectively, to bring about certain perlocution. A sample excerpt from W.W. Jacobs's 'The Monkey's Paw' (Jacobs W.W. in *Poetry and Minor Forms of English Literature*, ed. Oxford, 1998: 193-211) is assessed below, with a view to explore the operation of the non-locutionary means in the excerpt.

2.10 The excerpt from 'The Monkey's Paw'

MR. WHITE: I will ! [He holds up the paw, as if half ashamed]

I wish for two hundred pounds.

[crash on the piano. At the same instance Mr. White utters a cry and lets the paw drop.]

MRS. WHITE:
AND HERBERT: } What's the matter?

MR. WHITE: [gazing with horror at the paw]: It moved!

2.10.1 Analysis of the excerpt

The scene has certain **perlocution of menace**, which is developed here non-verbally by body language functioning in the context of this speech situation. **The body language, here, creates a logically graded illocutionary force in an incrementing sequence** to reach the perlocution of menace. The sequence of the force is as follows:

1. Mr. White's holding up of the paw
2. His expression of being half ashamed
3. His screaming (cry) accompanied by a crash on the piano
4. His letting the paw drop; and
5. His gazing at the paw with horror

The sequence of the illocutionary force non-verbally develops the menace. Due to the force, the utterances are sized, shaped and given the situational meaning. That is to say, the perlocution emerges from the non-locutionary means operating in this speech situation.

The significance of non-locutionary means is so much here that the perlocution is seriously damaged, if the functioning of the body language or the non-locutionary means is eliminated from this excerpt. That is to say, the perlocution of the menace comes very much out of the non-locutionary means in the excerpt. If the non-locutionary means are eliminated from the excerpt, the utterances lose:

1. The logical sequence between them
2. Their illocutionary force, and thereby
3. The perlocution of the menace itself

In such a case, the situation may give out an ambiguous or a paralysed or an absurd message.

This is proved so in the following part, where the same excerpt is studied by removing the stage directions and the punctuations from it. [Here, the stage directions, and the punctuation that suggest the intonation are eliminated from the excerpt to suggest the elimination of the non-locutionary means from the scene]

MR. WHITE:	*I will I wish for two hundred pounds*
MRS. WHITE AND HERBERT:	*hat's the matter*
MR. WHITE:	*It moved*

The answer '**it moved**' by Mr. White, to the question '**What's the matter?**' by Mrs. White and Herbert, does not convey any concrete message. **It moved,** in such a case, may mean:

1. The paw moved casually (what conveys no signal of the menace through it);
2. The paw moved and which is a pleasant experience of anticipating the two hundred pounds for which Mr. White had tried the paw-trick;
3. The paw moved Mr. White (to tears);
4. Something else, apart from the above.

In fact, it moved conveys the whole menace in this situation. However, the menace i.e. the perlocution is not lively exposed to the audiences' perception, when the non-locutionary means are eliminated from the scene. This highlights the significance of the non-locutionary means overall in this speech situation, and also proves that there are chances of some ambiguous interpretation, or misinterpretation, or multiple interpretations, or even absurdity, if the non-locutionary means do not play their role. It results into the violation of 'clarity principle' (Leech, 1983: 66). Here, the above cross-assessment sums up with the following conclusions:

1. The clarity principle is violated, if the non-locutionary means are eliminated from the present speech situation.
2. The non-locutionary means are an inseparable aspect of the speech situations in drama.
3. To eliminate the non-locutionary means from the speech situations in drama is to paralyze the very perlocution following the same.

The Austinian perspective on the types of speech acts brings out the above-discussed aspects of the speech acts. A Searlean perspective is discussed below, so as to throw light on some more aspects of the speech acts.

2.11 Searlean perspective on speech acts

Searle (1969) developed Austin's speech act theory, wherein he added some more speech acts along with some conceptions like the 'expressibility principle' (Searle, 1969). Searle's theory also develops on the note of language as action, and projects the speech acts as the basic or minimal units of linguistic communication. In this connection, Searle mentions, 'if my conception of language is correct, a theory of language is part of a theory of action, simply because speaking is a rule-governed form of behaviour.' (Searle, 1969: 17) Thus, to postulate language as action and speech as behaviour, Searle elaborates on his concept of linguistic communication in general and the speech acts in particular, as follows:. According to Searle:

> *The unit of linguistic communication is not, as has generally been supposed, the symbol, word or sentence, or even the token of the symbol, word or sentence, but rather the production or issuance of the symbol or word or sentence in the performance of the speech act. To take the token as a message is to take it as a produced or issued token. More precisely, the production or issuance of a sentence token under certain conditions is a speech act, and speech acts are the basic or minimal units of linguistic communication.* (Searle, 1969: 16)

As far as the speech situations in drama are concerned, on assessing Searle's and Austin's perspectives on the types of the speech acts, a common foundation is found laid for the study of non-verbal means of communication in drama. The 'non-locutionary' element from Austin's theory; and the 'behavioral' element in the issuance or the production of the speech acts, from Searle's theory; emerge a common ground for the assessment of the non-verbal means of communication in drama. Besides this, there are some other communicational aspects also in the study of the speech acts. According to Searle:

> *There are a series of analytic connections between the notions of speech acts, what the speaker means, what the sentence (or other linguistic element) uttered means, what the speaker intends, what the hearer understands, and what the rules governing the linguistic elements are.* (Searle, 1969: 21)

Considering the various communicational aspects and the series of analytic connections between them, it seems quite obvious that the study of the speech acts is not possible in isolation, and that it needs to be studied in an overall setup of the speech situations. Thus, the interrelation between the study of the speech situations and that of the speech acts becomes strongly justifiable.

After throwing light on the various communicational intricacies and the newer dimensions of the linguistic communication, Searle introduces some new speech acts. Searle assigns names to at least three distinct kinds of acts:

(a) *Uttering words* (morphemes, sentences) = performing *utterance acts.*
(b) *Referring and predicating* = *performing propositional acts.*
(c) *Stating, questioning, commanding, promising, etc.* = *performing illocutionary acts.* (Searle, 1969: 24)

After naming these acts, Searle traces the operational interrelation between them as follows:

> *. . . in performing an illocutionary act one characteristically performs propositional acts and utterance acts. Nor should it be thought from this that utterance acts and propositional acts stand to illocutionary acts . . . They are not means to ends; rather, utterance acts stand to propositional and illocutionary acts in the way in which, e.g., making an "X" on a ballot paper stands to voting . . . Thus, in performing different utterance acts, a speaker may perform the same propositional and illocutionary acts.* (Searle, 1969: 24)

Though Searle introduces some new acts as seen above, he develops the same on the basis of Austin's introduced speech acts, as stated earlier. It was not only Searle, who reviewed Austin's speech act theory, but many others like Leech (1983) also have reviewed the same in their own way. The Leechian perspective on the speech acts is discussed in the next chapter.

2.12 Conclusion

The chapter reviews the various theoretical conceptions related to the present research. The perspectives and the theoretical issues discussed in this chapter are used as a theoretical base to the analytical part of the study. The Leechian perspective on the 'aspects of speech situations' in particular is used as a base to evolve an analytical model required for the study. The next chapter 'Towards the Analytical Model' evolves the analytical model.

CHAPTER-3

TOWARDS THE ANALYTICAL MODEL

The structure of audio-visual texts like theatre performances requires a somewhat more elaborative inventory of analytical instruments than linguists usually provide. In particular, the old sender-receiver model of communication is too simple to explain the communicative relationship between the participants of dialogues presented to audiences in theatre plays.

(Earnest W B Hess-Luttich, 1991: 232)

3.1 Preliminaries

The present chapter proposes to evolve an analytical model to analyze the speech situations particularly in the print form of drama. As the 'analytical instruments'(Earnest W B Hess-Luttich, 1991: 232) provided by the linguists—for instance, Leech's 'aspects of speech situations' (Leech, 1983: 13-15)—satisfy the requirement of the proposed analysis but partially, the need for the new analytical model becomes justifiable. It is observed that certain parameters need to be evolved to pinpoint the various communicational intricacies in the script of drama.

The script of drama creates a communicational world, which is neither absolutely social, nor absolutely literary, nor absolutely theatrical, but includes all of them. The 'three worlds' (Popper, 1972), and the 'fourth world' (Leech, 1983: 52) are helpful in describing the dramatic communicational world of the script, to some extent. However, the above-referred four worlds have certain limitations to explicate the dimensions like the theatrical and the technological setup, operating as part of the ideational communication, in the script. Thus, the worlds of Popper (1972) and Leech (1983), as well as the branches of pragmatics like 'Socio-pragmatics[1], Textual Pragmatics[2]' (Leech, 1983: 63-70), and 'Literary Pragmatics[3]' (Mey, 1993: 236-261) can satisfy the requirements of the proposed analysis partially, what underlines the need for some appropriate new analytical model.

Considering the above-discussed limitations of the existing models, the study has proposed Model-1 in the chapter of Introduction. Model-1 provides some parameters of analysis with a view to satisfy the present analytical requirements; however, being only a hypothetical model, it needs some authentication. Hence, the study authenticates

Model-1, by assessing it against Leech's concept of the 'aspects of speech situations' (Leech, 1983: 13-15), what evolves the new analytical model.

Leech's concept includes the following aspects:

1) *Addressers or addressees*
2) *The context of an utterance*
3) *The goal(s) of an utterance*
4) *The utterance as a form of act or activity: a speech act*
5) *The utterance as a product of a verbal act* (Leech, 1983: 13-14)

Leech further mentions:

> *We can compose a notion of a speech situation, comprising all these elements and perhaps other elements as well, such as the time and the place of the utterance* (Leech, 1983:15).

It can be observed that Leech leaves his concept open ended. His accommodative approach shows certain scope for some newer components. The assessment of Model-1 against Leech's concept can uncover the possibilities of such components.

3.2 The assessment of Model-1

The assessment is aimed at evolving a new analytical model. The following objectives throw light on the line of assessment.

3.2.1 Objectives of the assessment

How and where the components of speech situations described by Leech are found functioning in Model-1.

Exploration towards the additional components, if any, in the composition or in the operation of the speech situations in Model-1.

The assessment initially undertakes the analysis of some sample speech situations from drama on the basis of the parameters in Model-1, and following it, the results of the analysis are assessed against Leech's concept, so as to authenticate the notion of the speech situations in Model-1. Precisely, with the help of the sample situations, the parameters in Model-1 are assessed against the parameters in Leech's concept. A sample from Karnad's *The Fire and the Rain* (Karnad, 1998) is analyzed below.

3.2.2 Sample-1

The following sample is taken from the act-1 of the play (Karnad, 1998: 18, 19).

> (*[sd1] Arvasu, confused, walks to his father's hermitage.*
>
> *Vishakha has gone to the hermitage ahead of Arvasu. She is about to enter the house when her father-in-law, Raibhya, steps out. He is thin and emaciated, but*

physically active. Vishakha is horrified to
see him. He scowls at her.)

RAIBHYA: [u1] Where were you all this while?

VISHAKHA: [u2] I—I'd gone—to fetch water.

(*[sd2] She has no pot with her.)

RAIBHYA: [u3] Really?

(*[sd3] Arvasu comes in with the pot of water
and is startled to see Raibhya.)

ARVASU: [u4] Father! I didn't know you were returning
home today—[p1]

RAIBHYA: [u5] I didn't either. But perhaps I should give the
two of you more such surprises.

(*[sd4] Arvasu puts the pot down in a corner
and retreats.)

3.2.3 Parameters in Model-1 and their manifestations in drama

Model-1			The excerpt
Parametrical components of the speech situation			**Manifestations in drama**
Composition of the speech situations	Compositional components	Addresser and addressee	The characters in the play	Raibhya, Vishakha and Arvasu
		Context	Emerges out of the stage directions and the dialogues	The stage directions: [sd1] to [sd4]; and the utterances: [u3] and [u5] in the excerpt evolve the context: Raibhya was not at home, and so the other two are surprised on his unexpected arrival.
		Message: <u>Conversational</u>	Written and mainly verbal	The above-mentioned stage directions and dialogues in the excerpt appear in the written and verbal form.
		<u>and Narrative</u>	The stage directions about the characters' body language, time, place etc.	The stage directions [sd1] to [sd4] revealing the body language are: - 'Vishakha is horrified.' - 'Raibhya scowls at her.' - 'Arvasu is startled to see Raibhya.' - 'Arvasu puts the pot down in the corner.' - 'Arvasu retreats.'

(Contd. from the previous page)

Model-1			The excerpt
Parametrical components of the speech situation			Manifestations in drama
Operation of the speech situations	Mode of operation	Transmission channel / Verbal and non-verbal (written form)	Verbal transmission: the dialogues in the excerpt. Non-verbal transmission: The body language of the characters suggested through the stage directions in the excerpt.
		Reception channel / Verbal and non-verbal (written form)	Characters' reception of the utterances, as a response to the above-mentioned transmission, before their turn taking, e.g. Raibhya's reception of [u2] and [sd2] includes both the verbal and the non-verbal reception, before he takes his turn [u3].
		Communication / Interpersonal	The interpersonal communication between Raibhya and Vishakha; and Raibhya and Arvasu.

The table shows the manifestation of both the composition and the operation of the speech situation, as stated hypothetically in Model-1. Thus, the hypothetical model practically validates its operational mechanism.

Although thus validated practically, Model-1 looks still rather rough and loosely described, since it doesn't clarify the compositional and the operational status of the components like the time of action, the place of action, the relationship between the interlocutors etc. The following part of the assessment concentrates on the same.

Prior to assessing Model-1 against Leech's concept, it cannot be ignored that drama is a literary genre, and so is the language used in it, and so are the speech situations in it. Hence, it should be settled, whether the literary speech situations in drama could be fore grounded against Leech's pragmatics-oriented concept, which is more applicable to the non-literary speech situations. To clarify his own view in this concern, Leech says:

I shall argue that foregrounding—significant literary 'deviation' against the background of a non-literary norm—is just as applicable to the pragmatic study of language in context as to other, more formal, aspects of language. (Leech, 1992: 259)

Besides the above argument, significantly enough, Leech (1992) himself has applied his theory (see Leech, 1992 in Toolan, 1992: 259-280) to a drama, G.B. Shaw's *You Never Can Tell* (Shaw, 1898).

Finding

On the basis of the above argument, the assessment of the literary speech situations in drama (Model-1) against Leech's concept becomes justifiable.

3.3 Model-1 against Leech's concept of speech situations

The present stage of the assessment has the following objectives.

To authenticate and conceptualize the notion of the speech situations.

To facilitate the pragmatic study of the speech situations from drama.

To pursue the earlier—proposed objectives:

How and where the components of the speech situations stated by Leech are found functioning in drama

To study, whether there are any additional components in the constitution and operation of the speech situations in drama than those postulated by Leech

The assessment begins with the compositional components, followed by the operational mechanism, as stated in Model-1. However, it should be cleared that Leech does not produce any distinction like the composition and the operation of the speech situations. The two levels are mentioned and distinguished here, according to Model-1, for the convenience of the assessment.

3.4 The assessment of the compositional components in Model-1

The compositional components in Model-1 are as follows::

1. Addressers and addressees
2. Context
3. Message (conversational and narrative).

The assessment makes the following observations:

1. The first component the addresser and addressee is common between Model-1 and Leech's concept.
2. The second component context is also common between the two.
3. As far as the third component message (conversational) in Model-1 is concerned, it coincides with the aspect, 'the utterance as a form of act or activity: a speech act' (Leech, 1983: 14) in Leech's concept, since both of them deal with the **use of language**. On pursuing further, it is observed that the use of the language in Model-1 and also in Leech's concept is not merely syntactic and semantic, but it has rather a pragmatic application, since Model-1 and Leech by the use of the language mean the **language in action** (see 3.2.3 for the use of the language and the body language) and the **language as action** respectively. According to Leech,

'An utterance may be a sentence-instance, or sentence-token; but strictly speaking, it cannot be a sentence.' (Leech,1983: 14)

Leech clearly denies the status of an utterance merely as a sentence in the syntactic and the semantic sense; moreover, he projects the utterance rather as an act or action. The component message in Model-1 is also projected as an act or action, as seen in 3.2.3. Precisely, the **act** or the **action** element in **the use of language** pragmatically evolves as a coinciding function between the component, message (conversational) in Model-1, and the aspect, utterance from Leech's concept.

4. The only remaining component in Model-1 is message (narrative) i.e. the use of the stage directions in drama. Leech's concept doesn't give place to an aspect like this, perhaps because Leech's concept is not dramatics-oriented, but pragmatics-focused. However, the aspect, 'the utterance as a form of act or activity: a speech act (illocutionary act)' (Leech, 1983: 14) in Leech's concept, coincides with the stage directions in drama. The illocutionary act is 'an act in saying something' (Austin, 1962: 120). The stage directions also operate 'in' communicating the playwright's message to the audiences i.e. they inform about the **act** or the **action** to be performed **in** communicating the dialogues, e.g. the role

of [sd3] in communicating Arvasu's surprise in [u4], as seen below.

([sd3] Arvasu comes in with the pot of water and is startled to see Raibhya.)

ARVASU: [u4] Father! I didn't know you were returning home today—[p1]

On the basis of the above manifestation, it is observed that the component, stage directions coincides with the aspect, illocutionary act, stated in Leech's concept. The following table shows the coinciding / non-coinciding between Model-1 and Leech's concept.

3.4.1 Coinciding / non-coinciding of the compositional components in Model-1 and Leech's concept

The following table throws light on the comparative view of Model-1 and Leech's concept. The arrow drawn between the points shows the coinciding between them. The observations emerging from the table are discussed below it.

Sr. no.	Model-1	Leech's Concept
1	Addressers and addressees ⟶	Addressers or addressees
2	Context ⟶	The context of an utterance
3	Message: Conversational (dialogues) Narrative (stage directions)	The goal (s) of an utterance
4	----------------------------	The utterance as a form of act or activity: a speech act
5	----------------------------	The utterance as a product of a verbal act

3.4.2 Observations

The assessment sums up with the following observations:

1. Serially, the first component in the table is apparently common between Model-1 and Leech's concept. However, what Model-1 calls addressers **and** addressees, Leech calls addressers **or** addressees. The difference between '**and**' and '**or**' needs some more exploration.

2. The same is the case with the serially second component in the table. What Model-1 calls broadly the context, Leech specifies as the context of an utterance. The scope of these conceptions also needs further comparative exploration.

3. Message: conversational and narrative, the third component from Model-1 coincides with the fourth aspect of Leech's concept, the utterance as a form of act or activity: a speech act.
4. The third and the fourth aspects of Leech's concept viz. the goal (s) of an utterance and the utterance as a product of a verbal act are found non-coinciding with Model-1.
5. On the basis of observation no. 4, it is found that Model-1 has either certain lacunae or certain scope for the further exploration towards its authentication.

The above observations explicate the coinciding / non-coinciding between Model-1 and Leech's concept at the compositional level.

The assessment continues with the operational mechanism in Model-1. The study of the operational mechanism in Model-1 is the study of how the above-assessed compositional components operate through the following operational modes: 1) Transmission channel 2) Reception channel, and 3) Mode of communication. At this stage, the assessment explicates the general operational mechanism followed by the component-wise operational mechanism.

3.5 The assessment of the general operational mechanism

The general assessment is a collective study of all the components of Model-1 against Leech's concept. On the basis of the sample analyzed earlier (see 3.2.3), it is observed that the <u>addressers and addressees</u>, in the given time, space, and in the <u>context</u>, communicate the <u>message</u> in the verbal and non-verbal form of the language, by operating through the <u>transmission channel</u> and the <u>reception channel</u>, in their <u>interpersonal communication</u>. Thus, all the components collectively play their respective roles in **the interpersonal communication**, which **emerges as the center of the general operational mechanism in Model-1.** Hence, the assessment of Model-1 against Leech's concept also centers on the interpersonal communication.

Like Model-1, Leech's concept is also centered on the interpersonal kind of communication, though the very first aspect of Leech's concept, addressers **or** addressees, apparently does not suggest an interpersonal kind of communication, but suggests either an addresser-centered **or** an addressee-centered single-ended communication. Leech names the aspect as the addressers **or** addressees, and not as the addressers **and** addressees. Regarding the naming of this particular aspect, the researcher holds the view that Leech wants to call attention also to the writer and the reader, who also operate respectively as the addresser and addressee, in the print form of communication, where the communication is not interpersonal completely, but partly personal and partly ideational (see 'the communicational performance in the print form of drama' discussed under 1.3.1 in the chapter of Introduction). Leech, in this connection, states:

> *I shall refer to addressers and addressees, as a matter of convenience, as **s** ('speaker') and **h** ('hearer'). These will be a shorthand for 'speaker (s)/writer(s)' and 'hearer(s)/ reader(s)'. Thus the use of the abbreviations **s** and **h** does not restrict pragmatics to the spoken language.* (Leech, 1983: 13)

After encompassing also the writer(s) and the reader(s), along with the speaker(s) and the hearer(s), under the scope of his conception of the addresser-addressee, Leech names his conception as the addressers **or** addressees, instead of the addressers **and** addressees. Leech here deliberately distinguishes the independent identity of the addresser from the addressee and vice versa, so as to suggest the independent operation of each of them in the absence of the other, i.e. the writer(s) operate as the addresser(s) normally in the absence of the reader(s)-addressee(s) and vice versa. However, by naming the aspect so, Leech doesn't mean here only one-way communication of either of the addresser(s)-addressee(s). In fact, Leech directs his concept of the speech situations towards a two-way kind of interpersonal communication, which is evident here and also in the other aspects of his concept, where both the addresser(s) and the addressee(s) operate together in the interpersonal communication. It is confirmed in his idea of context, where Leech states:

> *I shall consider context to be any background knowledge assumed to be shared by **s** and **h** and which contributes to **h's** interpretation of what **s** means by a given utterance.* (Leech, 1983:13)

Leech clearly mentions here the roles of both the **s** and the **h** i.e. the addressers and the addressees. This makes the communication interpersonal in its nature. While describing the remaining aspects also, Leech assumes the communication to be interpersonal in its nature.

Thus, it is observed that like Model-1, Leech's concept is also centered on the interpersonal communication. The following points clarify the same; moreover, the interpersonal communication emerges as the common and coinciding area between Model-1 and Leech's concept, as produced below:

Leech describes the goal(s) as the function of an utterance, operating between both the addresser(s) and the addressee(s), hence the communication is interpersonal.

The illocutionary act in his concept is described as, the utterance as a form of act or activity: a speech act, which of course needs the same two ends: the addresser(s) and the addressee(s), for its operation. So the communication is interpersonal.

The last aspect is described as, the utterance as a product of a verbal act, which hints at the reception and the response—the function coinciding with the perlocutionary act from Austin's 'Speech act theory' (Austin, 1962)—of the addressee(s), facilitated by the 'illocutionary force' (Leech, 1983:15). Here also the 'producer' of the utterance and the 'receiver' of the same are in the interpersonal communication.

Precisely, Leech's concept, like Model-1, is also centered on the interpersonal communication.

The interpersonal communication in Model-1 accommodates a collective functioning of all the components; and the same way the interpersonal communication in Leech's concept too accommodates a collective functioning of all the aspects.

Hence, on this ground, it can be stated that the general operational mechanism of the interpersonal communication in Model-1, and the same in Leech's concept, coincide with each other.

3.5.1 Finding

The interpersonal communication emerges as the common and coinciding area between the operating mode of the speech situations in drama (Model-1) and the speech situations in Leech's concept.

3.6 The component-wise assessment of the operational mechanism

After the general assessment, the present cotmponent-wise assessment proposes to study Model-1 against the aspect-by-aspect operation of Leech's concept, with a view to especially trace the non-coinciding operating mode, if any, between Model-1 and Leech's concept.

An investigation in response to the following questions can certainly help to trace the probable non-coinciding area. The questions are framed on the basis of the operation of every aspect from Leech's concept. In this sense, each aspect of Leech's concept gives out a different question.

Q.1) How far does the operating mode of addresser and addressee coincide / non-coincide with that of the components from Model-1?

Q.2) What is the scope of context in Leech's concept? How long does it coincide / non-coincide with the context in Model-1?

Q.3) Is the operation of the goal(s) in Leech's concept coinciding / non-coinciding, someway, with the operation of any of the components from Model-1?

Q.4) What measures does the illocutionary act coincide / non-coincide in its operation with the component(s) from Model-1?

Q.5) What's the scope of the operating mode of utterance in Leech's concept? How far does it coincide / non-coincide with that of the components from Model-1?

The concept of Leech is drawn from his theory of 'pragmatic principles' (Leech, 1983). Naturally, the above questions can properly assess the pragmatics-centered dimension of Model-1, and thereby trace the non-coinciding area, if any. The aspect-by-aspect assessment is worked out as follows:

3.6.1 Question-1

How far does the operating mode of the addresser and addressee coincide / non-coincide with that of the components from Model-1?

The conception of the operating mode of the addressers and addressees in general and its scope in particular should be clearly stated before its assessment. The following deliberation by Leech (1992) throws light on the present conception, its scope and the actual area of assessment under it.

While applying his theory to G B Shaw's comedy *You Never Can Tell* (Shaw, 1898), Leech says:

> *I assume, as part of this principle-constrained theory of pragmatics, that humans carry around with them a conception of what is a norm (in part societal, in part personal) of cooperative or polite behaviour for a given conversational situation. These norms are variable according to who the speakers are; what the social relations between them are; what the situational background in terms of what kind of activity they are engaged in is; what goods and services are being transacted; what the background presumptions regarding the rights and obligations of individuals are, and the relative weightiness of various rights and obligations, goods and services.*
> (Leech, 1992: 262)

Leech mainly deliberates on certain conceptual norms that influence the operating mode of the conversational behaviour of the users of language i.e. of the addressers and addressees. As the addressers and addressees operate through their conversational behaviour, the same emerges as their operational area and the assessment area as well. Hence, the assessment of the operating mode of the addresser and addressee concentrates on the assessment of their conversational behaviour, and the factors influencing the same. The changing conversational behaviour of the addressers' and addressees' in Leech's concept is assessed here against its Model-1 counterpart that evolves from the sample analyzed under 3.2.3.

In Model-1, the conversational behaviour of the addressers and addressees is explicated by the components like the stage directions, the context, the transmission channel, the reception channel etc. All these components holistically operate (see the operation of the context, the transmission channel, the reception channel etc. in 3.2.3) in the said explication, e.g. the conversational behaviour of Raibhya, Vishakha and Arvasu is explicated not by these addressers and addressees themselves alone, but mainly by the stage directions, the transmission channel, the reception channel etc., as produced in 3.2.3.

Precisely, the area of the conversational behaviour of the addressers and addressees in Leech's concept coincides with the holistic operation of the components like the addressers and addressees, the stage directions, the transmission channel and the reception channel from Model-1.

3.6.1.1 Findings

1. The operational area of the addressers and addressees in Leech's concept coincides with the operational area of the addressers and addressees, the stage directions, the transmission channel and the reception channel from Model-1.

2. No non-coinciding with regard to the addressers and addressees is found between Leech's concept and Model-1.

Besides the above findings, on the basis of the various types of dramatic performances it is also found that the component, addresser and addressee, operates in the various roles, which find place neither in Model-1 nor in Leech's concept. Hence, an explication regarding the unexplored roles of the same is produced below:

3.6.1.2 Unexplored roles of addressers and addressees

In the assessment of Model-1 against Leech's concept of speech situations, certain roles of the addressers and addressees remain unexplored. The various types of performances—viz. theatrical performance, radio performance, recorded audio-visual performance and so on—show that the role of the addressers and addressees undergoes certain variations depending upon the type of dramatic performance. For instance, the role of the playwright as an addresser, being the writer of a play and the role of the readers as addressees, being the readers of that play; also the role of the listeners of a radio performance as addressees, the actors' role as addressees while reading a play and their role changed as addressers while performing the same play, and the roles of the director, the technicians, the backstage artists as the addressers and addressees cannot be ignored, since all of the above mentioned addressers and addressees play vital roles in the different types of dramatic performances.

It is important to note here that neither Model-1, nor Leech's concept incorporate these various types of addressers and the addressees. Hence, the analytical model to be evolved needs to incorporate the following types of addressers and addressees in it:

3.6.1.3 Types of addressers and addressees

1. **Author-addresser:** the playwright.

2. **Performing-addressers:** the actors in the performance of drama.

3. **Reader-addressees:** the readers of drama.

4. **Viewer-addressees:** the spectators in the theatre.

5. **Tele-viewer-addressees:** the audience of the tele-visual performance of drama on the screen.

6. **Audio-addressees:** the audience of the radio-performance of drama.

7. **Performer-addressees:** the artists (actors, directors, music operator, lights operator, make-up-man, prompter, back-stage artists and so on), who read the play for the performance of their roles.

With the above discussion and findings the assessment under question-1 completes here. The question-2 and the part of the assessment related to it are produced below:

3.6.2 Question-2

What is the scope of the context in Leech's concept? How long does it coincide / non-coincide with the context in Model-1?

Leech (1983), with regard to the context says:

> *I shall consider context to be any background knowledge assumed to be shared by **s** and **h** and which contributes to **h's** interpretation of what **s** means by a given utterance.* (Leech, 1983:13)

In Leech's definition of context, the following are the two parts:

The context as any background knowledge assumed to be shared by the speaker and the hearer.

The context as a contributing factor in the hearer's interpretation of the utterance.

If the context, according to Leech, is any background knowledge assumed to be shared by the **s** and **h**, then 'the situational background in terms of what kind of activity the **s** and **h** are engaged in, and the background presumptions regarding the rights and obligations of the **s** and **h**' (Leech: 1992: 262) shared by the addresser and addressee should also be considered as the context.

On the basis of the above citations, as the context from Leech's concept proves to be such a wide area (as to accommodate the knowledge of the situational background of the activity between *s* and *h*, and also the background presumptions of the rights and obligations of *s* and *h*), the context in Model-1 needs to be assessed against the same wide scope of the context.

To assess Model-1 against the above-discussed scope of context in Leech's concept, the part of the sample excerpt analyzed under 3.2.3 is reviewed here.

3.6.2.1 Review of sample-1

(^sd1 _Arvasu, confused, walks to his father's hermitage._

Vishakha has gone to the hermitage ahead of Arvasu. She is about to enter the house when her father-in-law, Raibhya, steps out. He is thin and emaciated, but physically active. Vishakha is horrified to see him. He scowls at her.)

RAIBHYA: ^u1_Where were you all this while?_

VISHAKHA: ^u2 _I—_p1 _I'd gone—_p2 _to fetch water._ (^sd2 _She has no pot with her._)

RAIBHYA: ^u3 _Really?_ (^sd3_Arvasu comes in with the pot of water and is startled to see Raibhya._)

ARVASU: ^u4 _Father! I didn't know you were returning home today—_p3

RAIBHYA: ^u5 _I didn't either. But perhaps I should give the two of you more such surprises._ (^sd4 _Arvasu puts the pot down in a corner and retreats._)

3.6.2.2 Analysis

The analysis of the above sample is focused only on the operating mode of the context in it. The above sample brings out the operating mode as follows:

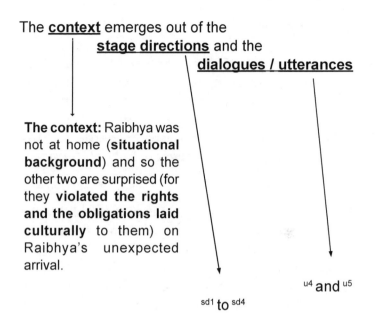

The **context** emerges out of the
stage directions and the
dialogues / utterances

The context: Raibhya was not at home (**situational background**) and so the other two are surprised (for they **violated the rights and the obligations laid culturally** to them) on Raibhya's unexpected arrival.

u4 **and** u5

sd1 **to** sd4

As the analysis shows it, significantly enough, the points: 1) the situational background; and 2) background presumptions regarding the rights and obligations of **s** and **h,** are found functioning through the context, the stage directions and the dialogues / utterances as well. On the basis of these observations, the assessment evolves the following findings.

3.6.2.3 Findings

1. The scope of the context, illustrated in Leech's concept, coincides with the context as well as the stage directions and the dialogues / utterances in Model-1.
2. No non-coinciding with regard to the context is found between Leech's concept and Model-1.

Besides the above findings, it is also found that the context operates in the socio-cultural, the literary and the theatrical dimensions in drama. These various dimensions find place neither in Model-1 nor in Leech's concept. Hence, the unexplored area of the context is produced below.

3.6.2.4 Unexplored dimensions of the context in drama

There are various dimensions of the context in drama, which remain unexplored in the above assessment. The socio-cultural, the literary and the theatrical dimensions of the context operate holistically in drama. For instance, the socio-cultural context of the folklore in Karnad's plays; the context of the literary devices like personification, imagery, symbolism and so on, in drama; and the theatrical context of the use of the lights, the music, the special costumes, the stage props and so on, in the theatrical performance, are some of the contextual dimensions, which are not explored in the above assessment of Model-1 against Leech's concept. Hence, the following dimensions of the context need to be incorporated in the new analytical model.

3.6.2.5 Contextual dimensions in the analytical model

1. Socio-cultural dimension of context
2. Literary dimension of context
3. Theatrical dimension of context

On the basis of the discussion under question-2, the study recommends that the above dimensions of the context should find place in the analytical model, especially when they find place neither in Model-1, nor in Leech's concept.

3.6.3 Question-3

Is the operation of the goal(s) in Leech's concept coinciding / non-coinciding someway with the operation of any of the components from Model-1?

Leech comments on the conception of the goal(s) of an utterance in his *Principles of Pragmatics* (Leech, 1983) as follows:

> *I shall often find it useful to talk of a goal or a function of an utterance in preference to talking about its intended meaning, or s's intention in uttering it. The term goal is more neutral than intention because*

> *it does not commit its user to dealing with conscious volition or motivation but can be used generally of goal-oriented activities.* (Leech, 1983: 13, 14)

The comment clearly focuses upon the goal-oriented activities (that are carried out along with the use of an utterance), rather than upon the user's intention behind the utterance. This becomes more explicit in Leech's (1983) further comment. According to Leech:

> *We cannot ultimately be certain of what a speaker means by an utterance. The observable conditions, the utterance and the context, are determinants of what s means by the utterance.* (Leech, 1983: 30)

After stating the observable conditions, the utterance and the context as the determinants of the goal(s) of an utterance, Leech comments on an important, and here, a relevant function of the general pragmatics:

> *General pragmatics relates the sense (or grammatical meaning) of an utterance to its pragmatic force.* Moreover he says: *The force will be represented as a set of implicatures.* (Leech, 1983: 30)

The ideas, the force and the implicature, mentioned above, are found clearly coinciding with each other, and together they coincide with Leech's conception of the goal(s); since the trio: the force, the implicatures and the goal(s), are related in the same way with the effect of the utterance; and also because they too are determined by the observable conditions, the utterance and the context. Regarding especially the implicatures, Grice (1975) also states, 'The presence of a conversational implicature must be capable of being worked out.' (Grice, 1975: 50)

Here, Grice emphasizes the point that the very existence of the implicature—which coincides with Leech's conception of goal(s)—can be determined only in its 'working out' i.e., in its operating mode. Leech says that the above remark of Grice's is 'A corollary of the claim that pragmatics studies behaviour that is motivated, in terms of conversational goals' (Leech, 1983: 30)

Here, the study of the behaviour is studying one of the observable conditions. As far as the speech situations in drama are concerned, the study of the behaviour is obviously the study of the body language used by characters, since this is one of the observable conditions [the other observable conditions can be the use of 'the artifacts' (Kachru Y., 1982), e.g. the stage property used by the characters]. If the body language of the characters is the part of the observable conditions, and if the same is suggested through the stage directions in the script of drama, it can be stated that **the stage directions emerge as one of the parameters of the study of the goal(s) of an utterance in drama.** This is where the operation of the goal(s) of an utterance, from Leech's concept, coincides with the operating mode of the stage directions in Model-1. However, the coinciding in this regard is not only with the stage directions but also with the two more Model-1 components, the context and the message, as Leech himself mentions the context and the utterance (a counterpart of the Model-1 component message in the present assessment) to be the determinants of the goal(s).

Summing up the discussion, Leech's conception of goal is found centered on the goal-oriented activities that are recognizable through the determinants of the goal(s), viz. the observable conditions, the context and the utterance. Pragmatically viewing, these determinants embody the pragmatic force, to which the sense of an utterance is correlated. The force and the implicatures are realized through the behavioural activities, so, the study of the goal(s), becomes the study of the behavioural activities, which are precisely studied in the 'means-ends analysis' (Leech, 1983: 40) in Leech's theory, where Leech conclusively says:

> *In short, the term goal is used in the neutral Artificial Intelligence sense of 'a state which regulates the behaviour of the*

individual' in such a way as to facilitate a given outcome. (Leech, 1983: 40)

On the basis of the above discussion, the assessment evolves an observation that **the goal is a state of regulating the behaviour.**

If the goal is the regulating state of the behaviour, and if the regulating state of the behaviour of the characters in drama is explicated by the stage directions, the context and the message in Model-1, the assessment evolves the following findings.

3.6.3.1 Findings

1. **The operating mode of goal(s) coincides with the operation of the Model-1 components, the stage directions, the context and the message.**
2. **No non-coinciding with regard to the goal(s) of an utterance is found between Leech's concept and Model-1.**

3.6.4 Question-4

What measures does the illocutionary act coincide / non-coincide in its operation with the operating mode of the component(s) from Model-1?

While illustrating the fourth aspect from his concept, the illocutionary act, i.e. the utterance as a form of act or activity: a speech act, Leech says, 'Pragmatics deals with language at a more concrete level than grammar.' (Leech, 1983: 14)

Though, basically Leech pinpoints the difference between pragmatics and grammar in the above remark, the concrete level, he refers to, is significant at the present stage of the assessment. The details of the concrete level are explicitly brought out in the following deliberation, which in a way hints at the operating mode of the illocutionary act.

> *Whereas grammar deals with abstract static entities such as sentences (in syntax) and propositions (in semantics), pragmatics deals with verbal acts or performances, which take place in particular situations, in time.* (Leech, 1983: 14)

The verbal acts or the performances taking place in the particular situations, in time, are nothing but the illocutionary act evolved by Leech, on analyzing and revising Austin's conception in the chapter: *'Speech-act verbs in English'* (Leech, 1983: 198-228). According to Austin, an illocutionary act is 'performing an act in saying something'. (Austin, 1962)

The acts performed in saying something are obviously some linguistic behaviour. According to Austin, the status of the linguistic behaviour is singular, whereas, Leech states it differently as,

'Linguistic behaviour is made up of complexes of activity, rather than of single events, . . . as in the means-ends model.' (Leech, 1983: 201)

Thus, the linguistic behavior—that includes the 'complexes of activity in saying something', i.e. the illocutionary act—precisely clarifies the operating mode of the illocutionary act in Leech's concept.

On the basis of Leech's above-given remarks, the operating mode of the illocutionary act clearly emerges as a behavioural or an action-centered operating mode. The same is observed even in his concept of the means-ends analysis, in which the **means** that take the communication process to the **ends** are mainly the verbal acts or the performances observed in the linguistic behaviour of the *s* and the *h*. The model depicts a speech situation in which the speaker feels cold; and **in** saying that he wants the hearer to switch on the heater by *means* of 'a' below (*s's* action of telling *h* to switch on the heater), his behavioral or the action-centered complexes of the activity (verbal and non-verbal) i.e. the **linguistic behaviour** plays the key role.

3.6.4.1 The means-ends model

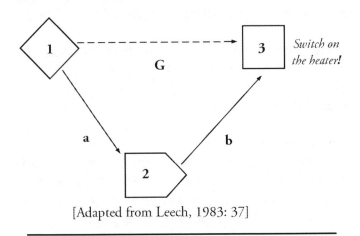

[Adapted from Leech, 1983: 37]

---

1 =   initial state (*s* feels cold)

2 =   intermediate state (*h* understands that *s* wants the heater on)

3 =   final state (*s* feels warm)

G =   goal of attaining state 3 (getting warm)

a =   *s's* action of telling *h* to switch on the heater

b =   *h's* action in switching on the heater

Leech's (1983) means-ends model cited above shows three states: 1) the initial state where the speaker's feeling cold is expressed; 2) the intermediate state, where the hearer understands that the speaker wants the heater on; and 3) the final state, where it is expressed that the speaker feels warm. G in the model is the goal of attaining the final state—i.e. getting warm—attained through 'a' (the speaker's action of telling the hearer to switch on the heater), and '**b**' (the hearer's action in switching on the heater).

In the given model '**a**' plays the most important role, as far as the operating mode of illocutionary act is concerned. Leech, himself, projects the same as the most important part of his model since, he had evolved the model basically to study 'the speaker's task, viewed in terms of means-ends analysis' (see Leech, 1983: 36). The '**a**' connects the **initial state** of the *s's* feeling cold through the verbal acts or the performances (the use of the language with some non-verbal bodily action like shivering) to the **intermediate state** of the *h's* understanding that *s* wants the heater on. The '**a**', thus, represents the speaker's linguistic behaviour or more precisely, the **operating mode of the illocutionary act** (what leads to the *perlocutionary* effect that will be studied later under question-5).

Precisely, on the basis of the above discussion, it is found that what Leech means by **the illocutionary act is not the single but the multiple means of the verbal and the non-verbal communication in an overall linguistic behaviour, that operates 'in' saying something**.

After the operating scope and mode of the *illocutionary act* from Leech's concept is studied, it is important to assess its coinciding / non-coinciding with the Model-1 components.

Since the illocutionary act is found operating through the verbal and the non-verbal means of communication, the Model-1 components dealing with such means need to be assessed against it. Hence, the assessment narrows down to the addresser and addressee, the stage directions and the message that operate the verbal and the non-verbal means through the transmission and the reception channel of the interpersonal communication in Model-1.

The speech situation in the following excerpt from Karnad's play, *The Fire and the Rain* (Karnad, 1998) shows the actual operating mode of the above-mentioned Model-1 components.

3.6.4.2 Sample-2

PARAVASU'S VOICE: [u1] *Arvasu*—$_{p1}$ *Arvasu*—$_{p2}$ (^{sd1}*Arvasu gets up. Runs to the hermitage. He sees Paravasu and Vishakha bending over something near a thicket.)*

PARAVASU: [u2] *Arvasu*—$_{p3}$ *here!* (^{sd2}*Plucks the arrow from Raibhya's body.)*

ARVASU: [u3] *Where are you?*

PARAVASU: [u4] *Here, near the neem tree.*

ARVASU: [u5] *What are you doing there?* (^{sd3}*He goes and finds Paravasu and Vishakha kneeling over Raibhya's body.)* [u6] *What is it? What has happened?*

Is that father? What happened to him? Oh God! Blood! Blood!—$_{p4}$ what's happened? Oh my God—$_{p5}$ I can't—$_{p6}$

PARAVASU: ^{u7}*In the dark, I—$_{p7}$ I mistook him for a wild animal—$_{p8}$*

3.6.4.3 Operational mode of the illocutionary act in Model-1

Model-1		The Excerpt	
Parametrical components of the Speech Situation		**Operational mode**	**Findings**
Composition of speech situations	**Compositional Components**	Addressers and addressees	Paravasu and Arvasu (also seen are Vishakha and the deadbody of Raibhya)	Verbal (dialogic) and non-verbal (behavioural)
		Context	Not a means-oriented factor here	Not assessed
		Message: <u>conversational</u> and <u>narrative</u>	Verbal: (^{u1} to ^{u7}) and Non-verbal: ($_{p1}$ to $_{p8}$)	Verbal: through utterances, and non-verbal: through punctuation marks e.g. the use of dash
			Stage directions:^{sd1} $^{to\ sd3}$ showing chronology, place of action, characters' body language, artifacts used e.g. the arrow in Raibhya's body etc.	Narrative, author directly communicating to readers/ actors /directors hence, not ideational totally

Operation of speech situations	Mode of operation			
		Transmission channel	Verbal:(u^1 to u^7) mainly between Paravasu and Arvasu; non-verbal: through $p1$ to $p8,$ and in $sd1$ to $sd3$ between all characters	Textual; Verbal: dialogic and Non-verbal: punctuation marks; Narrative in the stage directions
		Reception channel	— ,, —,, —,,—	— ,, — ,,— ,,—
		Communication	Interpersonal	Interpersonal
		Nature of data for assessment	Textual: an excerpt from the play	Not applicable

3.6.4.4 Findings

1) The operating mode of illocutionary act allows scope for the multiple means of communication and the complexes of activity in the linguistic behaviour.

2) Naturally, the means of communication emerge as the base of the assessment under 3.6.4 i.e. question—4.

3) The means of communication in Model-1 operate through the addressers and addressees, and the message.

4) Hence, the illocutionary act from Leech's concept coincides with the addressers and addressees fully; and with the message partially.

5) As the use of the artifacts is one of the non-verbal means of communication in drama (see Table-3.6.4.3), the stage directions, directing about the use of the

artifacts in Model-1, show some area in their operating mode that **non-coincides with the illocutionary act** from Leech's concept. It is quite obvious, since Leech has not included the use of the artifacts directly in his concept anywhere.

6) However, though he does not include the use of the artifacts directly, Leech leaves his concept open ended. In this connection, Leech mentions:

> *We can compose a notion of a SPEECH SITUATION, comprising all these elements, and perhaps other elements as well, such as the time and the place of the utterance.* (Leech: 1983: 15)

7) As Leech clearly inclines on including the time and the place of the utterance, **the use of the artifacts can certainly be included in the analytical model.** The inclusion is certainly justifiable on the following ground:

a) The 'means' have emerged as the very crux of Leech's conception of the illocutionary act.

b) Also, the 'means' have emerged as the common factor between Leech's concept and Model-1.

c) So the 'means' emerge as the very basis of the present assessment.

d) The operation of the artifacts in drama is found as the means-centered operation (see findings: 1, 2, 5; and Table-3.6.4.3 above). Hence, the inclusion of the same in the analytical model becomes highly justifiable, as an illocutionary usage.

Besides the above findings, on the basis of Austin's 'Speech Act Theory' (Austin: 1962), some other types and subtypes of the speech acts also manifest their applications in drama. The area of the speech acts operating in drama but not explored under the present assessment is explicated below.

3.6.4.5 Unexplored area of the speech acts in drama

Austin's (1962) speech act theory explores the various types and subtypes of the speech acts, viz. 'Locutionary speech act' (Austin, 1962: 94) and its subtypes the 'Phonetic act'(Austin: 1962: 95), the 'Phatic act' (Austin, 1962: 96) and the 'Rhetic act' (Austin, 1962: 95); also the 'Illocutionary speech act' (Austin, 1962: 120); and the 'Perlocutionary speech act' (Austin, 1962: 120). These speech acts operate in drama as follows:: The locutionary speech act finds its application in drama, since its subtypes, the phonetic act, the phatic act and the rhetic act operate respectively in the dialogue delivery, at the grammatical level and in the rhetorical usage. The illocutionary speech act operates in drama through the verbal as well as non-verbal acts, e.g. see the verbal acts in the utterances $u1$ to $u7$ and the non-verbal acts in the pauses $p1$ to $p8$, as analyzed under 3.6.4.2 The same sample also explicates the operation of certain verbal and non-verbal perlocutionary expressions.

For instance, $u4$ below is a **verbal perlocution** to$u3$.

> *ARVASU:* $u3$ *Where are you?*
> *PARAVASU:* $u4$ *Here, near the neem tree.*

And $sd1$ is a **non-verbal perlocution** to $u1$, and $p1$ and $p2$, as produced below.

PARAVASU'S VOICE: $u1$ *Arvasu—*$p1$ *Arvasu—*$p2$

($sd1$ *Arvasu gets up. Runs to the hermitage . . . .*

On the basis of the above explication, it is found that there are certain types and subtypes of the speech acts, which operate in drama but find place neither in Model-1 nor in Leech's concept. Hence, the study recommends incorporating these speech acts in the analytical model. The recommended speech acts are listed below:

3.6.4.6 Types and subtypes of the speech acts in drama

i) <u>**Locutionary speech act**</u>:
   a) **Phonetic act:** the phonetic level, e.g. the voice modulation in the dialogue delivery
   b) **Phatic act:** the syntactic level
   c) **Rhetic act:** the semantic level

ii) **Illocutionary speech act**: the verbal and the non-verbal (kinesic, paralinguistic, and proxemic) forces

iii) **Perlocutionary speech act**: the verbal and the non-verbal (kinesic, paralinguistic, and proxemic) expressions

3.6.5 Question-5

What's the scope of the operating mode of the utterance as a product of a verbal act in Leech's concept? How far does it coincide / non-coincide with that of the Model-1 components?

The utterance is one of the very important aspects of Leech's concept of speech situations. Leech describes it as the 'utterance as a product of a verbal act' (Leech, 1983: 14), where he states, 'When we try to work out the meaning of an utterance, . . . thus the meaning of an utterance, in this sense, can be called its ILLOCUTIONARY FORCE.' (Leech, 1983: 14, 15)

Leech describes the utterance as the illocutionary force and also as the product of a verbal act, since the utterance, in the form of the illocutionary force, operates at the **product stage,** out of the various stages, of a verbal act. Leech, thus, specifies the operating scope of the utterance especially to the product stage and calls utterance a product: the illocutionary force. Regarding the meaning of the illocutionary force and especially to distinguish it from the illocutionary act, Leech states, 'Illocutionary force is the communicative plan or design behind s's remark . . . and the illocutionary act is the fulfillment of that communicative goal.' (Leech, 1983: 200)

If the utterance is called the illocutionary force, and if the illocutionary force is the communicative plan, then the operating scope of the utterance can be seen stretched back from the earlier discussed **product stage** to the **plan stage** of a verbal act. In addition to this, Leech clearly describes even the fourth aspect of his concept, the illocutionary act, as 'the utterance as a form of act or activity: a speech act' (Leech, 1983: 14). Here, the operating scope of the utterance—which thus functions through the act or the activities—can also be seen spread even between the plan stage and the product stage of the verbal act. That means, the operating scope of the utterance, the last aspect of Leech's concept, encompasses the area from the communicative plan stage in *s's* mind, through the middle stage, the act / activity, to the product stage of a verbal act.

Precisely, according to Leech's concept of the speech situations, the utterance, the fifth and last aspect of his concept, is found operating at the three different stages.

1) The (communicative) plan;
2) The act / activity; and
3) The product.

However, out of these three stages, the scope of the first stage, plan, is already accommodated and studied in the operating mode of the goal(s) (the third aspect of Leech's concept), which is called 'a neutral artificial intelligence sense of a regulating state (here the plan) of an individual's (s's) behaviour' (Leech, 1983: 40). So, it is not necessary to study the plan stage of an utterance under the operating scope of the utterance (the fifth aspect in Leech's concept). Apart from this, even the scope of the next stage, the act / activity, is already accommodated and studied in the operating mode of the illocutionary act (the fourth aspect in Leech's concept), which is described as 'the utterance as a form of act or activity: a speech act' (Leech, 1983: 14). So, like the exclusion of the plan stage of an utterance, even the study the middle stage, the act / activity form of an utterance, needs to be excluded from the operating scope of the utterance (the fifth and the last aspect of Leech's concept).

The above discussion explicitly shows that the first two stages of the operating scope of the utterance are already encompassed under the earlier discussed two aspects of Leech's concept, the goal(s) and the illocutionary act, so these stages need to be excluded from the study of the utterance.

So, the assessment, on the basis of this discussion emerges the following finding:

3.6.5.1 Finding

Leech narrows down the operating scope of the utterance—the fifth and the last aspect of his concept of speech situations—only to the product (of a verbal act: illocutionary force) stage of the verbal act.

After the above finding evolves, the assessment hereafter explores yet another pragmatic dimension of the utterance. Leech, at the very outset of his theory states:

> *I present a complementarist view of pragmatics within an overall programme for studying language as a communication system . . . . This conception of communication leads to a rhetorical approach to pragmatics.*
> (Leech, 1983: x,xi)

In accordance with his rhetorical approach to pragmatics, and the complementarist view, Leech further clarifies his conception of the illocutionary force, which has emerged as the very crux of the utterance. He distinguishes between the **illocutionary force** and the **rhetorical force** and at the same time clarifies their bilateral *complementary*[4] roles in the pragmatic sense of the term. Leech mentions:

> *Together the illocutionary force and the rhetorical force of an utterance make*

> *up its PRAGMATIC FORCE . . . . The*
> *distinction between SENSE (meaning as*
> *semantically determined) and FORCE*
> *(meaning as pragmatically determined)*
> *is essential to this study. But it is also*
> *essential to realize the bond between*
> *the two: force includes sense and is also*
> *pragmatically derivable from it.* (Leech,
> 1983: 17)

Leech's views, cited above, help in exploring and evolving the pragmatic dimension of the utterance. Pragmatically viewing, Leech describes the utterance as the illocutionary force, and in the above cited views, rhetorically viewing, Leech states that the force includes the sense. If the force includes the sense and if the 'utterance produces the illocutionary force' (see Leech, 1983: 15) then, this becomes clear that the utterance also—as it is called the illocutionary force (the meaning determined pragmatically)—includes the SENSE (the meaning determined semantically) in its FORCE, which is pragmatically derivable and determinable too.

Precisely, both the sense and the force are inclusive in Leech's conception of the utterance. Hence, the present assessment accordingly explores the pragmatics (the force) as well as the semantics (the sense) of the utterances in drama. So, Model-1 is assessed here against Leech's conception of the utterance, by means of assessing the following sample taken from Karnad's *The Fire and the Rain* (Karnad, 1998).

3.6.5.2 Sample-3

NITTILAI: (^{sd1}*Pause.*) ${}_{p1}$
$\qquad$ ^{u1} *And have you faced your own people?*
Told them yet?
(^{sd2} *No reply.*) ${}_{p2}$
^{u2} *You haven't* ${}_{\backslash\,fi\text{-}1}$, *have you? Do you feel ashamed?*

ARVASU: ^{u3} *Ashamed? Let me show you—* ${}_{p3}$ *here!*
(^{sd3} *Grabs her hand and pulls her near.*)

NITTILAI: ^{u4} (^{sd4} *Scandalized*) *Let go of me! Let me go! What'll everyone say?*

ARVASU: ^{u5} ${}_{(ri\text{-}1)\,/}$ *Why? Don't I have my* ${}_{(ri\text{-}2)\,/}$ *rights—* ${}_{p4}$ *?*

NITTILAI: ^{u6} *Not* ${}_{(n1)}$ *until* ${}_{(n2)}$ *we are married. Until* ${}_{(n3)}$ *then the girl is not* ${}_{(n4)}$ *supposed to touch her husband— to-be. That's our custom—* ${}_{p5}$

---

^{u} = Utterance	${}_{p}$ = Pause
^{sd} = Stage direction	${}_{ri}$ = Rising intonation
${}_{n}$ = Negation	${}_{fi}$ = Falling intonation

In the above sample the utterances ${}^{u1,\ u2,\ u3}$ and ^{u4} give out their ***force*** respectively through a pause (see ${}_{p1}$), a no reply (see ${}_{p2}$), body language directed (see ^{sd1}), and some physical expression of a mental state (*scandalized Nittilai*, see [sd4]). The utterance $u5$ gives out its **force** through the pause (see $_{p4}$) and the rising intonation (see $_{ri-1 \text{ and}}$ $_{ri-2}$). The utterance $u6$ gives out **an incrementing force** of refusal, **functioning in an ascending order** and **structured in a syntactic sequencing** of repeated negation (see $_{n1, n2, n3 \text{ and } n4}$) followed by an affirmative sentence: *"that's our custom"*, and lastly a pause ($_{p5}$) strongly exhibiting the force of refusal against an anti-cultural demand in $u5$. It is the syntactic sequence of 1) repeated negation; followed by 2) an affirmative sentence; preceding 3) a highly communicative pause, what makes the utterance $u6$ very much distinctive from the other utterances. These ***pragmatic forces,*** given out by the utterances $u1$ to $u6$, along with their nature and communicative mode are categorized below.

3.6.5.3 Analysis of the operation of the utterance (pragmatic force) in Model-1

Utterance	The force given out	Communicative mode of the force	Nature of the force	Operating Model-1 component
U1	Suspicion	Pause ($_{p1}$)	Non-verbal	Message: narrative ([sd1])
U2	Suspicion asserted with a blame	'No-reply' response ($_{p2}$)	Non-verbal	Message: narrative ([sd2])
U3	Male chauvinism	Body language ([sd3])taking place in a pause ($_{p3}$)	Non-verbal	Message: narrative ([sd3]) and co-textual˙ / grammatical($_{p3}$)

U4	Feminine feeling of being scandalized	Some gesture (not specified in the script)	Non-verbal	Message: narrative (^{sd4})
U5	Askance for a cultural right	Rising intonation ($_{RI\ 1}$ and $_{ri\text{-}2}$) and a pause ($_{p4}$).	Verbal (^{u5}); paralinguistic ($_{ri\text{-}1}$ and $_{ri\text{-}2}$) and non-verbal ($_{p4}$)	Message: conversational (^{u5}) and co-textual / grammatical ($_{ri\text{-}1,\ ri\text{-}2}$) and ($_{p4}$)
U6	Refusal to the mistaken cultural right	Syntactic sequencing of an ascending force of negation ($_{n1,\ n2,\ n3\ and\ n4}$) in the utterance, and a pause ($_{p5}$)	Verbal (syntactic sequencing $_{n1,\ n2,\ n3\ and\ n4}$) and non-verbal ($_{p5}$)	Message: conversational ($_{n1,\ n2,\ n3\ and\ n4\ in}$ ^{u6}) and co-textual / grammatical ($_{p5}$)

* *Co-textual* (see Crystal, 1980: 114)

The above table analyzes the operation of the utterances and the Model-1 components involved in the operation. Message emerges as the main Model-1 component in this operation. The operating mode of the utterance, as a product of the verbal act, coincides mainly with the Model-1 component message and also with the transmission channel, the reception channel and the type of communication in drama. The assessment under 3.6.5 gives out the following findings:

3.6.5.4 Findings

The operating scope of the utterance as a product of the verbal act coincides with the operating scope of the Model-1 components: the message, the transmission channel, the reception channel and the type of communication.

No non-coinciding with regard to the utterance as a product of the verbal act is found between Leech's concept and Model-1.

With the above findings, the assessment of Model-1 against Leech's concept completes here. The assessment evolves the following major areas of findings:

1. The operational area of speech situations coinciding between Leech's concept and Model-1.

2. The operational area of speech situations non-coinciding between Leech's concept and Model-1.

3. The operational area of speech situations found neither in Model-1, nor in Leech's concept, but in the actual speech situations in drama.

3.7 Coinciding area between Leech's concept and Model-1

On the basis of the findings under 3.4, 3.4.1, 3.4.2, 3.5.1, 3.6.1.1, 3.6.2.4, 3.6.3.1, 3.6.4.4, 3.6.5.1, and 3.6.5.4, the assessment evolves the following operational area of the speech situations coinciding between Model-1 and Leech's concept.

Sr. no.	Leech's Concept: Aspects of speech situations	Model-1: Components
1	'Addressers or addressees' Coincides with	1. Addressers and addressees (as per 3.4) 2. **Message** (as per 3.6.1.1) 3. Transmission channel (as per 3.6.1.1) 4. Reception channel (as per 3.6.1.1)
2	'The context of an utterance' coincides with:	1. Context (as per 3.4. & 3.6.2.4) 2. **Message** (as per 3.6.2.4)
3	'The goal (s) of an utterance' coincides with:	1. Context (as per 3.6.3.1) 2. **Message** (as per 3.6.3.1)
4	'The utterance as a form of act or activity: a speech act' coincides with:	1. **Message** (as per 3.4 & 3.6.4.4) 2. Addressers and addressees (as per 3.6.4.4)
5	'The utterance as a product of a verbal act' coincides with:	1. **Message** (as per 3.6.5.4) 2. Transmission channel (as per 3.6.5.4) 3. Reception channel (as per 3.6.5.4) 4. Communication (as per 3.6.5.4)

3.7.1 Finding

The above table emerges message as the common component from Model-1, and which coincides with the every aspect of Leech's concept of the speech situations.

3.8 Non-coinciding area between Leech's concept and Model-1

On the basis of the findings under 3.4.1 and 3.4.2 the assessment evolves the following operational area of the speech situations non-coinciding between Model-1 and Leech's concept.

Sr. no.	Leech's Concept: Aspects of speech situations	Model-1: Components
1	'Addressers or addressees'	No non-coinciding found
2	'The context of an utterance'	No non-coinciding found
3	'The goal (s) of an utterance'	Does not coincide with Model-1 as per the general assessment under 3.4.1 and 3.4.2. However, coincides with the Context (as per 3.6.3.1) and with the Message (as per 3.6.3.1) in the component-wise assessment.
4	'The utterance as a form of act or activity: a speech act'	No non-coinciding found

| 5 | 'The utterance as a product of a verbal act' | Does not coincide with Model-1 as per the general assessment under 3.4.1 and 3.4.2. However, coincides with the Message (as per 3.6.5.4); the Transmission channel (as per 3.6.5.4); the Reception channel (as per 3.6.5.4) and the Communication (as per 3.6.5.4); |

3.8.1 Finding

Although the above table shows that 'The goal (s) of an utterance' and 'The utterance as a product of a verbal act' from Leech's concept non-coincide with Model-1, at the level of the general assessment; the same are found coinciding with certain Model-1 components at the component-wise assessment.

The following table explicates the details in the above finding:

Sr. no.	Model-1	Leech's Concept
1	Addressers and addressees—→	'Addressers or addressees'
2	Context ————————→	'The context of an utterance'
3	Message: Conversational (dialogues) Narrative (stage directions)	No coinciding found
4	Transmission channel	No coinciding found
5	Reception channel	No coinciding found
6	Communication	No coinciding found

3.9 Unexplored area of the speech situations in drama

On the basis of the findings under 3.6.1.3, 3.6.2.6 and 3.6.4.6, the assessment finds out certain components, e.g. the use of the artifacts (see 3.6.4.3 and 3.6.4.4), which operate neither in Model-1, nor in Leech's concept. Hence, the study recommends the incorporation of the use of the artifacts as well as the following components under 3.9.1, 3.9.2 and 3.9.3 in the analytical model.

3.9.1 Types of the addressers and addressees

1. **Author-addresser:** the playwright.
2. **Performing-addressers:** the actors in the performance of drama.
3. **Reader-addressees:** the readers of drama.
4. **Viewer-addressees:** the spectators in the theatre.
5. **Tele-viewer-addressees:** the audience of tele-visual performance of drama on the screen.
6. **Audio-addressees:** the audience of radio-performance of drama.
7. **Performer-addressees:** the artists (actors, directors, music operator, lights operator, make-up-man, prompter, back-stage artists and so on), who read the play for the performance of their roles.

3.9.2 Dimensions of the context in drama

1. Socio-cultural dimension of context
2. Literary dimension of context
3. Theatrical dimension of context

3.9.3 Types and subtypes of the speech acts in drama

i) **Locutionary speech act:**

   a) **Phonetic act:** the phonetic level, e.g. the voice modulation in the dialogue delivery;
   b) **Phatic act:** the syntactic level;
   c) **Rhetic act:** the semantic level;

ii) **Illocutionary speech act:** the verbal and the non-verbal (kinesic, paralinguistic, and proxemic) forces;

iii) **Perlocutionary speech act:** the verbal and the non-verbal (kinesic, paralinguistic, and proxemic) expressions

On the basis of the assessment of Model-1 against Leech's concept of the speech situations in general and the recommendations under 3.9.1, 3.9.2 and 3.9.3 in particular, the chapter evolves the following analytical model. The model is centered on Message, since the same evolves as the central component as per 3.6.5.3, 3.7 and 3.7.1. The analytical model 3.10 shows the delimited area of the proposed analysis and also the parameters of the analysis.

3.10 The analytical model

AREA OF ANALYSIS

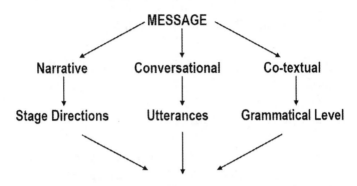

MESSAGE

Narrative   Conversational   Co-textual

Stage Directions   Utterances   Grammatical Level

PARAMETERS OF ANALYSIS

1. **Addressers and Addressees:**
   i) **Interpersonal**: characters in conversation;
   ii) **Ideational**: author-addresser[1], performing addressers[2] reader-addressees[3], viewer-addressees[4], tele-viewer-addressees[5], audio—addressees[6], performer-addressees[7], etc.)

2. **Context:**
   i) Socio-cultural dimension
   ii) Literary dimension
   iii) Theatrical dimension

3. **Speech-acts:**
   i) Locutionary act:
      a) Phonetic;
      b) Phatic: use of grammar;
      c) Rhetic: semantic level;
   ii) Illocutionary act: verbal and non-verbal (kinesic, paralinguistic, and proxemic) forces;
   iii) Perlocutionary act: verbal and non-verbal (kinesic, paralinguistic, and proxemic) expressions.

3.11 Conclusion

The present chapter basically aims at evolving the analytical model, with a view to explore the speech situations in the print form of drama. The analytical model is evolved here by assessing Model-1 against the 'aspects of speech situations' derived by Leech (1983). As a result of the assessment, the 'Message' emerges as the central component from Model-1. Hence, the analytical model also centers on the same, and vividly explicates the area and the parameters of the proposed analysis.

CHAPTER-4

ANALYSIS

Once we realize that what we have to study is not the sentence but the issuing of an utterance in a speech situation, there can hardly be any longer a possibility of not seeing that stating is performing an act. (Austin, 1962: 138)

4.1 Preliminaries

The analysis in this chapter is tuned to Austin's above-mentioned remark, with an assumption that a literary text of drama—besides the other performances of drama, viz. the theatrical performance, the recorded performance, the radio performance and so on—is also a performance in itself.

The present chapter analyzes the speech situations in the literary performances of drama. The analysis of the speech situations in the literary performance of drama has its own scope and limitations. The data of analysis appears here mainly in the form of three different areas of communication: conversation, narration, and co-text, through which all the components of the speech situations operate. These three areas together are named message in Model-1. As all the components of speech situations operate through the conversation, the narration, and the co-text, i.e. through the message, the component message emerges as the central component of the analysis, whereby all the other components too can be analyzed. As a result, the scope of the analysis is centered on the message.

Precisely, to analyze a speech situation, here, is to analyze the central component message, whereby it is possible to analyze collectively all the remaining components of the speech situations, viz. the addresser and addressee, the context, the speech acts etc., as mentioned below in the analytical model. The model produces the area of analysis and the actual parameters of analysis in the diagrammatic form, as follows:

4.2 The analytical model

AREA OF ANALYSIS

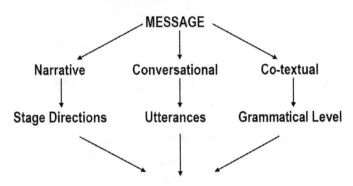

MESSAGE

Narrative   Conversational   Co-textual

Stage Directions   Utterances   Grammatical Level

PARAMETERS OF ANALYSIS

1. <u>Addressers and Addressees</u>:
   i) **Interpersonal**: characters in conversation;
   ii) **Ideational**: author-addresser[1], performing addressers[2] reader-addressees[3], viewer-addressees[4], tele-viewer-addressees[5], audio—addressees[6], performer-addressees[7], etc.)
2. <u>Context</u>:
   i) Socio-cultural dimension
   ii) Literary dimension
   iii) Theatrical dimension
3. <u>Speech-acts</u>:
   i) Locutionary act:
      a) Phonetic;
      b) Phatic: use of grammar;
      c) Rhetic: semantic level;
   ii) Illocutionary act: verbal and non-verbal (kinesic, paralinguistic, and proxemic) forces;
   iii) Perlocutionary act: verbal and non-verbal (kinesic, paralinguistic, and proxemic) expressions.

4.2.1 Terms used in the analytical model

The following terms are used in the analytical model. The use of these terms is original here, as they are not taken from any external source. Hence, it is essential to clarify their scope and meaning, which is mentioned against the terms.

---

[1]**Author-addresser**: the playwright.

[2]**Performing-addressers**: the actors in the performance of drama.

[3]**Reader-addressees**: the readers of drama.

[4]**Viewer-addressees**: the spectators in the theatre.

[5]**Tele-viewer-addressees**: the audience of the tele-visual performance of drama on the screen.

[6]**Audio-addressees**: the audience of the radio-performance of drama.

[7]**Performer-addressees**: the performers (actors, directors, music operator, lights operator, make-up-man, prompter, back-stage artists and so on), who read the play for its performance.

The analytical model produced above explicates both the area and the parameters of the proposed analysis. With the help of this model, the analysis of the speech situations from the selected plays is worked out partly in the present chapter and partly in the next chapter.

The present chapter undertakes the analysis of the speech situations from three plays, *Naga-Mandala* by Girish Karnad (1990), *The Dread Departure* by Satish Alekar (1989) and *Evam Indrajit* by Badal Sircar (1989). On the basis of the communicational variation, the speech situations are selected for the analysis. In all two samples are taken from each play. The analysis begins with *Naga-Mandala.*

4.3 Naga-Mandala: analysis

The play *Naga-Mandala* has a variety of speech situations. The communicational variety of the situations emerges from many a component, like the context of Indian folklore in the play. The play is summarized below, with a complementary illustration on the socio-cultural context of the Indian folklore.

4.4 About Naga-Mandala

Karnad's *Naga-Mandala* is an amalgam of two Kannada folk-tales. The first is a tale of the oral 'Tales'—personified in the play—that exist for ages independently (independent of a writer) and yet depend upon a story-teller to keep them alive by passing on to the other story-teller. The dependence and the independence of the tales bring out the paradox of the very nature of the oral tales. Interwoven with the first, in the play, the other tale is a tale of Rani, who remains absorbed in the tales, so as to replace her predicament of the real world by the enjoyment of the fictional world. Both these tales in the play bring in a folklore element that eventually evolves the very basic human character of juxtaposing the real and the fictional worlds.

4.4.1 Indian folklore as the socio-cultural context

The two Kannada tales, the 'tale of Tales' and also the 'Rani's tale' in the play, emerge from the Indian folklore, which, like in Karnad's other plays, also operates in this play, as the context, in which the communication in the play in general and the speech situations, or to narrow down further, the speech acts in particular are processed. As the socio-cultural ethos in the Kannada tales is part of the Indian folklore, and as the folklore is the part of the play, **the Indian folklore, by becoming the socio-cultural context of the communication in the play, operates as a connecting factor between the real world and, the literary and the theatrical worlds.** Basically, the folklore emerges from the real i.e. the 'societal world' (see 'The Three World Theory', Popper, 1972: 117; and its extension 'The Four World Theory', Leech, 1983: 52), and then operates as the socio-cultural context of the communication in the literary and the theatrical worlds, as seen in this play.

The emergence of the Indian folklore, as the socio-cultural context, is doubtlessly supported by the very concept of the folk theatre, which very often brings together the folklore and the theatre, the combination skillfully exercised by Karnad.

The folk theatre frequently brings together the traditional socio-cultural values in the folklore, the various literary techniques (like introducing the comic interludes and the amalgam of human and non-human worlds) in literature, and the various theatrical conventions (like the use of music, chorus, costumes, light effects etc) in the theatrical performances. With regard to this, Karnad himself says:

> *The energy of folk theatre comes from the fact that although it seems to uphold traditional values, it also has the means of questioning these values . . . The various conventions—the chorus, the music, the seemingly unrelated comic interludes, the mixing of human and non-human worlds—permit a simultaneous presentation of alternative points of view . . . They allow for, to borrow a phrase from Bertolt Brecht,* (Brecht, in Karnad, 1990) *"complex seeing".* (Karnad, 1990: cover page)

By and large, with the support of Brechtian 'complex seeing', and Karnad's view on the same, it is obvious that by influencing the literary as well as the theatrical expression, the context of the Indian folklore influences the entire process of communication in the play and thereby the speech situations, and ultimately also the speech acts, which, being 'the basic or minimal units of linguistic communication' (Searle: 1969: 16), and being the 'actual phenomenon' (Austin, 1962: 147) exchanged between the interlocutors, are an inseparable unit of the speech situations and thereby of the entire process of communication in the play.

The samples from Karnad's *Naga-Mandala* are analyzed below on the basis of the parameters mentioned earlier in the analytical model (see 4.2) showing the area and the parameters of analysis. All the samples follow the same pattern of analysis. The analysis begins with an assessment of sample-1 as follows:

4.5 Sample-1 (Prologue: p. 03)

The play opens with this sample. The Man's address '*to the audience*' and the device of personification are the special dramatic aspects of this situation.

MAN: ([sd1] To the audience) [u1] I had heard that when lamps are put out in the village, the flames gather in some remote place and spend the night together, gossiping. So this is where they gather!

> *([sd2] A new Flame enters and is enthusiastically greeted.)* (ibid.3)

The above part of the sample has two stage directions and one utterance considered for the purpose of analysis. The sample continues below:

FLAME 1: [u2] *You are late. It is well past midnight.*

NEW FLAME: [u3] *Ah! There was such a to-do in our house tonight.*

FLAMES: [u4] *What happened? Tell us!* (ibid…)

The three dialogues produced above are used as openers of narration. A story is narrated thereafter. The characters are good examples of personifications.

NEW FLAME: [u5] *You know I have only an old couple in my house. Tonight the old woman finished eating, swept and cleaned the floor, put away the pots and pans, and went to the room in which her husband was sleeping.* (ibid…)

New Flame starts narration of the story. It continues as follows:

And what should she see, but a young woman dressed in a rich, new sari step out of the room! The moment the young woman saw my mistress, she ran out of the house and disappeared into the night. The old woman woke her husband up and questioned him. But he said he knew nothing. Which started the rumpus. (ibid…)

The above narrative is used as utterance number five. It's a metaphorical tale that makes the Flames curious. Hence they interact as follows:

FLAMES: ^{u6}*But who was the young woman? How did she get into your house?*

NEW FLAME: ^{u7}*Let me explain: My mistress, the old woman, knows a story and a song. But all these years she has kept them to herself, never told the story, nor sung the song. So the story and the song were being choked, imprisoned inside her.* (ibid…)

Some important features of the oral literature and the narrative tradition are discussed here metaphorically. The following part of the utterance brings it out very well.

This afternoon the old woman took her usual nap after lunch and started snoring. The moment her mouth opened, the story and the song jumped out and hid in the attic. At night, when the old man had gone to sleep, the story took the form of a young woman and the song became a sari. (ibid…)

Personifications of the 'song' and the 'story' evolve the essence of oral literature here. The narrative continues below:

The young woman wrapped herself in the sari and stepped out, just as the old lady was coming in. Thus, the story and song created a feud in the family and were revenged on the old woman.

FLAME 1: ^{u8}*So if you try to gag one story, another happens.* (ibid…)

Some significant features and observations are produced below.

4.5.1 Sample 1: features and observations

• The sample is part of the prologue in the play
• One speech situation with two speech events ($^{sd1\ \&\ u1;}$ and ^{sd2} to ^{u8})
• The use of folklore as the context
• The characters: human and nonhuman (artifacts personified)
• The ambience: suspended between fantasy and reality

4.5.2 Sample-1: analysis

1. Addressers and Addressees

   a) Interpersonally operating

      Man, Flame-1, New Flame, and Flames operating from ^{u1} to ^{u8}.

   b) Ideationally operating

      i) Directly Ideational (directly from the author to the audience):

      The author-addresser addressing the reader-addressees and the performer-addresees e.g. as in ^{sd1} and ^{sd2}.

      ii) Indirectly Ideational (indirectly from the author to the audience, through the characters):

      The author-addresser addressing through Man's address '*To the audience*', as in ^{sd1}; and the characters (the interpersonally operating addressers and addressees) exchanging all the utterances from $u1$ to $u8$ to convey the author-addresser's message to the reader-addressees, the viewer-addressees, the tele-viewer-addressees, the audio-addressees, the performer-addressees and so on.

2. Context

i) Socio-cultural Dimension:

This dimension operates through the social beliefs (see $u1$ *'I had heard that . . . .'*) regarding the supernatural beings (here the Flames personified) and the communication between them.

Indian folklore, thus, by becoming the socio-cultural context of the communication in the play, operates as the connecting factor between the real world and, the literary and the theatrical worlds.

ii) Literary Dimension:

In this dimension the operation is observed through the literary conventions—like the personification (here of the Flames), the mixing of fantasies with reality, and the characters' communication with the audiences (in $sd1$)—known to all the addressers and addressees. The audiences' shared knowledge of the literary conventions operates as the literary dimension of the context.

iii) Theatrical Dimension:

The operation of this dimension is not mentioned in the stage directions, yet the place of action (*'some remote place'* in the village) and the time of action (*'the night . . . . when lamps are put out in the village'*) are stated in ᵘ¹ clearly, so as to propose the **use of the stage property** that sets up the remote place in the village (place of action).

The use of the light effects establishes the light and the very existence of the Flames; and also the darkness of the night (the time of action), in the context of which the speech in this situation can process in its theatrical performance.

3. Speech acts
i) <u>Locutionary act</u>

a) Phonetic act: A primary stress on the interjection *'Ah!'* in ᵘ³, expressing the weariness of New Flame, is a phonetic act noticed through the use of the exclamatory mark, following the interjection here.

The two examples of an obviously falling tone executed in ᵘ⁴ by all Flames; one at the end of the Wh-question *'What happened?'*, and another at the end of the imperative sentence *'Tell us!'*, are some more phonetic acts to mention here.

Finding

The phonetic acts are brought out by the use of the grammatical devices (the phatic acts).

> **b) Phatic act:** The phatic act operates here as the use of the grammatical devices (locution), e.g. the interjection followed by a punctuation (exclamatory) mark determining the (illocution) weariness of New Flame in [u3]; and the sentence types (the Wh-question and the imperative sentence) in [u4], and (the two Wh-questions) in [u6], determining the (illocution) excitement of all Flames to know the further part of the New Flame's narration of the 'Story'.

Finding

The phatic acts mentioned here operate as a linking factor between the locution and the illocution of the concerned utterances.

> **c) Rhetic act:** e.g. The act of explanation in [u7], and the act of conclusion in [u8] include the rhetoric skills of illustration and condensation of information, respectively to bring out the author-addresser's message— that the oral tales originate unstoppably independent of a certain author—through the utterance [u8] '*So if you try to gag one story, another happens*'.

Finding

In the performance of the rhetic acts mentioned above, the author-addresser emerges as the chief addresser, whereas the interpersonal interlocutors (here, all Flames and Man) remain instrumental (and thus perform some illocutionary function) in the process of the message transmission.

ii) Illocutionary act

Verbal Forces: e.g. the force of enquiry in [u2], the force of weariness in [u3], and the force of curiosity in [u4] and [u6] come out verbally.

The force of enquiry in [u2] is an <u>implicature of enquiry</u> (by the other Flames regarding New Flame's late coming), which operates as <u>questioning through statements</u>, and it is confirmed in the turn taking of New Flame in [u3], where she answers the enquiry by telling the reason for the delay.

Finding

The force of enquiry is an implicature of enquiry, operating as questioning through statements, and confirmed in the turn taking.

> **b) Non-verbal Forces** (kinesic, paralinguistic, and proxemic): e.g. the force of enthusiasm and greeting in the welcoming of New

Flame by the other Flames that operates <u>kinesically</u> (the assumed bodily expression of the greeting by Flames) and <u>proxemically</u> (the space distancing of New Flame) in ^{sd1}; and the force of weariness in ^{u1} operating <u>paralinguistically</u> through the interjection '*Ah!*'.

Some non-verbal acts like the kinesic, the proxemic and even the paralinguistic operations mentioned above can be obviously assumed and taken for granted, even though the same is not mentioned in the stage directions.

Finding

Certain non-verbal acts can be obviously assumed, even though the same is not mentioned in the stage directions.

iii) Perlocutionary act

a) Verbal Expressions: e.g. New Flame's verbal response (of answering the enquiry of all Flames regarding her late coming) in ^{u3} is a perlocution that all Flames expect (by implicating their enquiry) in ^{u2}; New Flame's verbal response (of narrating to all Flames) in ^{u5} is a perlocution that all Flames expect (by asking New Flame to narrate '*What happened*' with her) in ^{u4}; New Flame's verbal response (of explaining the details of certain part of her narration) in ^{u7} is a perlocution that all Flames expect (by asking New Flame the curious questions) in [u6] etc.

b) Non-verbal Expressions (kinesic, paralinguistic, and proxemic)**:** e.g. The proxemic responses of New Flame (by entering and space distancing), and the non-verbal expression of greeting by all Flames exchanged in [sd2], operate as the perlocution to an indirect command (of performing the perlocutionary acts of New Flame's entry and her welcome by other Flames for audiences) by the Man in his address *To the audience'* in [sd1]. The New Flame's paralinguistic response: *'Ah!'* (expressing her weariness) in [u3] is a very strong perlocution (expressing the genuine force of reasons behind her late coming and used as a part of her explanation) to the enquiry in [u2] by all Flames.

The acts in [sd2] are perlocutionary because they happen as the effects of Man's indirect command to New Flame and the other Flames (who are the performer-addressees because they receive the command, and also the performing-addressers because they act to the command), however the same acts also have an illocutionary function, as they operate 'in' (Austin: 1962: 120) conveying the Man's address *'To the audience'* [(sd1)].

Finding

The perlocutionary acts at the interpersonal level of communication (between Man and the other characters in this situation) have illocutionary functions at the ideational level of communication (between the author-addresser and all the audiences).

4.6 Sample-2 (act-2: p. 21-22)

This sample is about the meeting of Rani and Naga. The entire situation is processed in the context of fantasy and reality. Appanna (Rani's husband) keeps a watchdog to avoid any adultery by Rani, despite which Naga meets her.

> (*[sd1]She has fallen asleep against his chest. He slowly unties her hair. It is long and thick and covers them both. He picks up her hair in his hand, smells it.)*

NAGA:[u1] What beautiful, long hair ! Like dark, black, snake princesses! ([sd2] He lays her down gently. Gets up. Goes to the bathroom, turns into his original self and slithers away. (ibid. 21)

The above stage directions and utterance number one open this situation. Snake imagery is a significant feature of this sample.

[sd3]*Morning. Rani wakes up, and looks around. No husband. Comes to the front door. Pushes it. It is*

still locked. Baffled, she washes her face, goes to the kitchen and starts cooking. (ibid…)

The time of action mentioned in the above stage direction suggests change in the speech situation.

(^sd4 *The dog starts barking. Appanna comes. Pats the dog.*)

APPANNA: ^u2 *Hello friend! No intruders tonight, eh?* (^sd5 *He unlocks the door and steps in. At the noise of the door, Rani comes out running. She is laughing.*)

RANI: ^u3 *But when did you go away? I'm . . .* ~p1 (^sd6 *Freezes when she sees the expression of distaste on his face.*) (ibid…)

The interpersonal relationship can be judged from the above part. The following utterances are influenced by the very relationship

APPANNA: ^u4 *Yes?*

RANI: ^u5 *Oh! Nothing.*

APPANNA: ^u6 *Good* (^sd7 *Goes to the bathroom. Rani stares after him, then returns to the kitchen.*)

RANI: ^u7 *I must have been dreaming again—*~p2 (ibid…)

A psychological suspension of Rani is clearly seen in the above utterances.

([sd8]*Appanna bathes, then eats silently as usual and leaves. It grows dark. Night. Rani lies in the bed, wide awake. A long silence. The Cobra comes out of the ant-hill and enters the darkened front yard of her house. The dog suddenly begins to bark.* (ibid…)

The stage direction [sd8] indicates change of time and of the action. The animal imagery is a significant device used here.

…Then, sounds of the dog growling and fighting, mixed with the hiss of a snake. The racket ends when the dog gives a long, painful howl and goes silent. Rani rushes to the window to see what is happening. It is dark. She cannot see anything. When silence is restored, she returns to her bed. (ibid…)

The change of time again indicates the change of the speech situation here. It is important to study the changing shades of Rani's character, as the communicational partner changes.

[sd9] *The Cobra enters the house through the drain and becomes Naga. In the bathroom, he washes blood off his cheeks and his shoulder and goes to Rani's room. When she hears his step on the stairs, she covers her head with the sheet. Naga comes, sees her,*

> *smiles, sits on the edge of her bed. Waits. She peeps out, sees him, closes her eyes tight.)* (ibid. 22)

The stage direction number nine develops the context in which the following utterances are processed.

NAGA: [u8] *What nonsense is this? (*[sd10] *Without opening her eyes, Rani bites her forefinger. Gives a cry of pain.)* [u9] *What is going on Rani?*

RANI: ([sd11]*Rubbing her finger.)* [u10] *I must be going mad.*

NAGA: [u11]*Why?* (ibid…)

A linking between the physical and the psychological worlds of Rani is established by the logical linking of the utterances and the stage directions in the above part.

RANI: ([sd12]*To herself.)* [u12]*His visit last night—*[P3] *I assumed I must have dreamt that. I am certainly not dreaming now. Which means I am going mad. Spending the whole day by myself is rotting my brain.* (ibid…)

Rani's dilemmatic state of mind is depicted here. It's a beautiful blending of reality and fantasy.

NAGA: [u13]*It is not a dream. I am not a figment of your imagination either. I am here. I am sitting in front of you. Touch me. Come on! You won't? Well, then. Talk to me. No? All right. Then I had better go.*

RANI: ^{u14}*Don't.*$_{P4}$ *Please.* (ibid…)

The speech and the actions in the above sample very well coordinate with each other. This makes the situation meaningful.

4.6.1 Sample 2: features and observations

- The sample has three speech situations (^{sd1} to $^{sd2;}$ ^{sd3} to $^{sd8;}$ and ^{sd8} to $^{u14.}$)
- Every speech situation has the same place of action but different times of action that distinguish the situations from each other
- The characters are both natural (human) and supernatural (nonhuman)
- The human incarnation of the animal characters (*Cobra* as *Naga*)
- The communication between a human being and an animal (^{sd4} and ^{u2})
- The context of folklore
- The ambience of blending the fantasy and the reality

4.6.2 Sample-2: analysis

1. **Addressers and Addressees**
   a) **Interpersonally operating**
      Naga, Rani, and Appanna (see ^{u1} to ^{u14}); Dog appears as an addressee (^{u2}) operating

for Appanna, as Appanna's own tendency personified.

b) <u>**Ideationally operating**</u>

i) Directly Ideational (directly from the author to the audience):
The author-addresser addresses (^{sd1} to ^{sd12}) the reader-addressees and the performer-addressees

ii) Indirectly Ideational (indirectly from the author to the audience, through the characters):
The author-addresser addresses the reader-addressees and the performer-addressees through the characters' exchange of the utterances (^{u1} to ^{u14}).

2. Context

i) **Socio-cultural Dimension:**
The socio-cultural dimension of the context operates through the beliefs in the society, as observed in the sample, e.g. the human incarnation of Naga

ii) **Literary Dimension:**
The literary dimension rhetorically operates in the sample, e.g. the set of the adjectives, in ^{u1} in the context of which the illocutionary force of amour is processed and communicated to Rani.

iii) **Theatrical Dimension:**

All the utterances and the entire situation are processed in the context created by use of music, light effects, stage property etc.

The use of music, e.g. in creating the sounds like Dog's barking (^{sd4}) and growling (^{sd8}), Snake's hissing (^{sd8}).

The use of lights, e.g. to create effects of morning (^{sd2}), daylight and darkness of night (^{sd8}).

The use of stage property, e.g. the ant-hill (^{sd8}) and the house ($^{sd2, sd3, sd4, sd5, sd7, sd8, sd9}$).

3. Speech acts

i) <u>Locutionary act</u>

a) Phonetic act: An obvious rising tone is assumable as operating in the actual physical execution of the questions in ^{u4} by Appanna, and also in ^{u11} and ^{u13} by Naga. It is noticed through the use of the question marks, whereby the phatic act is observed to be complementary to the phonetic act in its operation.

b) Phatic act: The use of punctuations, e.g. the question marks in $^{u4, u11,}$ and ^{u13}; the pauses indicating no locution by the use of dots and dash ($_{p1 \text{ to } p4}$); the exclamations in ^{u1} communicating the emotional intensity, in

[u2] communicating a greeting of hello, and in [u5] communicating a surprise etc. These grammatical items help analyzing the type of locution and also the illocution in them.

c) Rhetic act: The rhetorical operation of a set of five adjectives in [u1,] and the appeal in the skill of persuasion in [u13] by conditioning, threatening a little etc.

ii) Illocutionary act

a) **Verbal Forces:** The force of amour in [u1] and the force of persuasion in [u13] operate as the illocutionary verbal forces.

b) **Non-verbal Forces** (kinesic, paralinguistic, and proxemic):
The force of amour operating kinesically in [sd1], Rani's cry of pain in [sd10] paralinguistically expresses the force of pain and a revelation of truth that she is in her senses. The [sd5] proxemically displays Rani's force of excitement and joy, when she comes out running.

iii) Perlocutionary act

a) **Verbal Expressions:** e.g. Rani's verbal response (of assuring her abiding to Appanna's set behavioural norms for her) in [u5] is a perlocution that Appanna expects (by questioning the very fidelity of hers to his rule) in ^{u4} and confirms in ^{u6}. Rani's verbal response (of succumbing to Naga's conditions and threats of persuasion) in ^{u14} is an anticipated effect of the force of persuasion in ^{u13}.

b) Non-verbal Expressions (kinesic, paralinguistic, and proxemic): e.g. The manifestations of the non-verbal perlocutionary expressions are Rani's <u>kinesic responses</u> in ^{sd2} to Naga's expectation of love making; the Dog's <u>paralinguistic response</u> of giving '*a long, painful howl*' and going '*silent*' suggesting his death in ^{sd8}, as a result of Cobra's punishment to him for blocking his way.

Also in ^{sd8}, '*Rani rushes to the window to see what is happening*', is a non-verbal perlocution that comes out of a <u>proxemic response</u> to the fight between the Dog and the Cobra.

With the above sample, the analysis of the speech situations from *Naga-Mandala* completes here. The next play selected for study is Satish Alekar's *The Dread Departure* (Alekar, 1989). The play is summarized below.

4.7 The Dread Departure: analysis

The samples selected from the play *The Dread Departure* are analyzed here. The analysis is worked out at the backdrop of the whole action in the play. The following section summarizes the action in the play.

4.7.1 About The Dread Departure

The Dread Departure (Alekar: 1989) is based on the theme of death. The thematic core effectively comes out through the device of the mourning *keertan*, a traditional Marathi art form. The play opens with the death of Bhaurao and the whole action is about his delayed cremation and the diverse human reactions to it. The cremation delays due to Bhaurao's strong wish of cremating his body, the way he wants and no other way. His body stinks, yet he doesn't allow the cremation. Meanwhile, Bhaurao's soul interacts with his wife Rama and the son Nana. As per his father's last wishes, Nana finally cremates his dead father in the old crematorium, after a long waiting and fighting against the civic rules. Until the cremation, Bhaurao's widow remains suspended between the love and the agony of her ghostly lover, '*the third from the left*' of the pall bearers. The play offers a cross-section of the societal and familial reactions on the death of Bhaurao. The following remark on the play voices the very crux of it.

The play has a rich dose of black humour, pure fun, and the sense of a community coming to terms with death. (ISBN 81, 7046, 059 X, in Alekar, 1989: cover page)

The selected samples from the play are analyzed below. The sample-1 is taken from the act-1, whereas the sample-2 is from the act-2 of the play.

4.8 Sample-1 (act-1: p. 18-19)

The present sample shows the neighbours of Bhaurao gathered for his funeral. Tired of waiting for Nana's arrival, they start playing the game of *'Last letter starts the rhyme'*. The situation changes after Nana's arrival. The sample offers fun and satire together in it.

> *(*[sd1] *Bier centre-stage. The man-on-the ladder still to one side. Neighbours divide themselves into groups for 'Last letter starts the rhyme'. Each side has a leader who 'conducts'.)* (ibid. 18)

The game of *'Last letter starts the rhyme'* is a manifestation of absurdity in this drama.

LEFT GROUP: [u1] *Come all ye faithful,*
　　　　　　Joyful and triumphant,
　　　　　　Come, all come to Bethlehem.
　　　　　　M! M! (ibid…)

It's a paradoxical view of death and recreation placed in one situation. The two groups play the game of *antakshari* around the bier.

RIGHT GROUP: [u2] *Michael, row the boat ashore.*
Hallelujah!
Michael, row the boat ashore, Hallelujah!
Sister, help us with the oars, Hallelujah!
A! A! (ibid…)

'*Hallelujah*' is a rhyming expression used to add rhythm and cheer up the participants in the game.

LEFT GROUP

LEADER: [u3] *Of course not! It's 'H'.*
Hallelujah. ([sd2] *Spells it out.*)
I have seen it in the dictionary!
([sd3] *They squabble about it.*) (ibid…)

The debate taking the last letter 'A' or 'H' is a common scene in such games. The game, at the backdrop of the death, trivializes one's death.

RIGHT GROUP

LEADER: [u4] *All right! H.*

LEFT GROUP: [u5] *Hark, the herald angels sing*
A new king born today.
Mary's boy child Jesus Christ
Was born on X'mas day.
Y! Y! (ibid…)

The death and the reference of birth in the song again intensify the paradox in this situation.

RIGHT GROUP

LEADER: [u6] *Y? Y? (*[sd4] *They confer and begin with)*
You are my shepherd, Lord! ([sd5] *And the other group joins in.)*
You are my saviour,
You are my shepherd, Lord,
You'll gather me in. (ibid…)

The threat of death and the pleading for protection are seen in the above part very well. Though apparently the game seems to be recreation, in fact it's an attempt of overcoming the threat and escaping from the same.

> (*[sd6] *As their singing becomes more and more loud and emotional, the man-on-the-ladder gets down. His eyes are full of tears and face alight with happiness. He tries to tell them something but his words are drowned out. In the end he puts two fingers in his mouth and whistles shrilly. They all stop. A moment of total silence* [p1] *while they all look at him. He speaks the following words to a drum beat and all join in.)* (ibid…)

The stage direction cited above is used as a device linking the earlier part of situation with the following utterances.

MAN ON LADDER: [u7] *Here is Nana*
       Home in haste.

ALL: [u8] *Home in haste.*
       Home in haste.
       Tired from playing
       Prisoner's base, home in haste. (ibid…)

The song clearly comments on the happenings around. In this sense, it emerges as a narrative. It narrates the happenings like 'Nana joins the group'. The song thus does not remain a casual part of the game. It establishes a linkage with the reality around.

> (*[sd7] They sing this while dancing faster and faster until all suddenly stop. Nana enters. Good-looking young man. Simply but well-dressed. They all surround him, trying to console, trying to hold and pat him. He is confused. Doesn't know what's going on. Pushes them away and sees the bier. A moment's silence [p2]. Then all neighbours again attack him and on a jazzy beat each one 'tags' him and consoles with him, playing 'Prisoner's Base'. Then:*) (ibid. 19)

The game of *'anatakshari'* becomes a metaphorical narrative of the occasion of death in this situation.

NEIGHBOUR 1: [u9] *This is a terrible thing. Yes, terrible. But what can one do? What can't be cured must be endured. That's the luck of the draw and you must play it, as it lays.*

NEIGHBOUR 2: [u10] *Who would have thought It? He was hale and hearty. To go like this and so suddenly. It's our loss and misfortune. This is a tough time, but you must be strong.* (ibid…)

Consolation on the death of a near and dear one is brought about metaphorically here.

NEIGHBOUR 3: [u11] *How could this happen to you? How could death choose yours?*

NEIGHBOUR 4: ([sd8] *cannot speak, can only bellow* [u12] *'Nana!' emotionally and play the 'tag').*

([sd9] *All exit after Nana.)* (ibid…)

Some of the significant features and observations regarding this sample are produced in the following part.

4.8.1. Sample 1: features and observations

- The sample has two speech situations (from [sd1] to [sd7] and from [u9] to [sd9])

• The sample blends the fun and the satire
• The versified utterances
• The gimmicky use of the *'Last letter starts the rhyme'*

4.8.2 Sample-1: analysis

1. Addressers and Addressees

a) Interpersonally operating

'Left group, Right group, Left group leader, Right group leader, Man on ladder, Neighbours1 to 4, Nana, and *Soul of Bhaurao'* (see [u1] to [u12]).

Nana operates only as an addressee in the verbal and the non-verbal communication of other addressers' (see [sd7, sd8, sd9,] and [u9 to u12]), whereas he operates as an addresser in his own non-verbal communication: e.g. in [sd7] *'He is confused. Doesn't know what's going on. Pushes them away and sees the bier. A moment's silence* (also see [p1] and [p2])' etc. The soul of Bhaurao through the theatrical techniques like dramatic irony (as suggested through the *'Bier centre-stage'* in [sd1]) operates here, as an addressee (and throughout the play he narrates and comments on the situations, as an addresser)

The theatrical gimmicks (here the presence of Bhaurao's soul suggested through the *'Bier centre-stage'* in [sd1]) and certain conventions like the 'dramatic irony' and the 'aside' throw light on some new dimensions of the component addresser and addressee. The very role of Bhaurao's soul as an addresser and addressee operating through the gimmicks and certain conventions, as stated above, evolves a new dimension like a supposed virtual addresser and addressee who operates physically.

Finding

The theatrical gimmicks and certain conventions like the 'dramatic irony' and the 'aside' evolve a new dimension: the supposed virtual 'addresser and addressee', who operates physically.

b) ### Ideationally operating

i) **Directly Ideational (directly from the author to the audience):**

The author-addresser addresses ([sd1] to [sd9]) the reader-addressees and the performer-addressees, e.g. about the contrast of the sound effects in [sd7], *'They sing this while dancing faster and faster* **(high-volume sound)** *until all suddenly* *stop* **(silence)**.*'* and *'*A *moment's silence.* **(silence)** *Then all neighbours again attack him and on a jazzy beat* **(high-volume sound)**.*'*

Also by directly addressing (stage direction) about the space distancing in *'playing'* the *'Prisoner's Base'* in [sd7], it seems that, the author-addresser dramatically (by interweaving the literary and the theatrical techniques) draws certain striking parallels between the game of *'Last letter starts the rhyme'* (chaining up the rhymes by the *'Last letter'* as said in [sd1]) and the game of the *'Prisoner's Base'* (chaining up the turns in the game by 'tagging' as said in [sd7]) and also the 'funeral process' (chaining up the earthly existence with the Heavenly existence by the cremation of Bhaurao's dead body) in this situation.

Findings

1. The author-addresser directly influences the theatrical performance by instructing about the sound effects and, about the actions and the space distancing of the actors (the performing addressers).

2. Thus by directly influencing the theatrical performance the author-addresser juxtaposes the literary and the theatrical

performances and thereby also key controls these performances.

ii) **Indirectly Ideational (indirectly from the author to the audience through the characters):**

The author-addresser addresses the reader-addressees and the performer-addressees through the characters' exchange of utterances ($u1$ to $u12$) and also their non-verbal communication in the same. The author-addresser here communicates his message to the audience by using a certain set of characters interchanging their roles, e.g. the Neighbours (1 to 4) also play the part of Left group or Right group or All to follow the playwright's plot.

Finding

The interchangeability of the characters' roles proves their being instrumental at the discretion of the author-addresser in the overall communication process from the author to the audience.

2. **Context**

i) **Socio-cultural Dimension:**

The socio-cultural dimension operates here as the beliefs in the society, e.g. the life after death, the existence of soul etc.

The rituals after death in the Hindu religion like the funeral and the cremation offer the context, wherein Bhaurao's death and his appearance as a soul become meaningful and acceptable throughout the play and in this speech situation in particular.

ii) Literary Dimension:

The literary dimension of the context operates through the techniques in the plot construction, e.g. the interweaving of the game of *'Last letter starts the rhyme'* (chaining up the rhymes by the *'Last letter'* as said in [sd1]) and the game of the Prisoner's Base (chaining up the turns in the game by 'tagging' as said in [sd7]) and the funeral process (chaining up the earthly existence with the Heavenly existence by the cremation of Bhaurao's dead body) in this situation.

iii) Theatrical Dimension:

All the utterances and the entire situation are processed in the context created by the use of music, light effects, stage property etc.

The use of music, e.g. the use of the drum beats as indicated in [sd6] and the jazzy beats as indicated in [sd7] in the singing and dancing (sd7) at the *'Last letter starts the rhyme'* (sd1); also the use of the chorus and the rhythm created through it, as observed in u1, u2, u5, u6, u8; an effective use of the utterance *'Hallelujah !'* in u2 in producing certain rhythmic effect, the musical effect of the *'shrill whistle'* causing the *'total silence'* in sd7 etc.

The use of body language, (acting) e.g. in the *'Last letter starts the rhyme'* (sd1), in playing the Prisoner's Base (sd6), and in Nana's confused (sd7) state of mind and his silent (Nana speaks nothing in this situation) behavioural communication (from u9 to u12 Neighbours talk to Nana, who remains silent and lastly exits, as seen in sd9).

The use of stage property, e.g. the bier and the ladder mentioned in sd1 remain in the performance throughout this situation. All the communication in this situation becomes meaningful in the context of Bhaurao's death, what is visually realized by the bier. The very presence of the bier is suggestive of the omnipresence of Bhaurao's soul that remarkably influences the communication throughout this play. The use of the ladder (and also of the binoculars) helps establishing the space and the distance of the place of action, from the road Nana is supposed to arrive by.

3. Speech acts

i) <u>Locutionary act</u>

a) Phonetic act: The use of chorus in [u1, u2, u5, u6] and [u8] obviously suggests certain rhythmic intonation pattern, as the tone of the whole chorus is supposed to be the one and the same.

The same is observed also with the forceful execution of the utterance, '*Hallelujah!*' in [u2].

The execution of the [u12] '*Nana!*' is directed to be not '*speaking*' but '*bellowing*' as per [sd8]: (*cannot speak, can only bellow 'Nana!' emotionally . . . .*)

b) Phatic act: The use of the punctuations e.g. at the end of [u1, u2] and [u5], the exclamatory mark is used to indicate the turn taking in the '*Last letter starts the rhyme*'; the utterance '*Hallelujah!*' in [u2] takes the exclamation for the recurring rhythm of the chorus, whereas, '*I have seen it in the dictionary!*' in [u3] takes it for the force of confirmation. The various applications of the exclamatory marks help perform various locutions.

c) Rhetic act: The literary technique of the intervention of poetry ([u1, u2, u5, u6, u7,] and [u8]) in drama is a rhetic act that makes the utterances emotionally more expressive, and so, more effective. The tragic situation (Bhaurao's death) in drama reflects effectively in poetry.

ii) Illocutionary act

a) **Verbal Forces:** e.g. the force of confirmation: *'I have seen it in the dictionary!'* in [u3]; and the force of emotional upsurge, *'Nana!'* (*'cannot speak, can only bellow . . . emotionally'*) in [u12] etc.

b) **Non-verbal Forces** (kinesic, paralinguistic, and proxemic): e.g. the force of consolation operates kinesically, by means of the game, the Prisoner's base in [sd7]; the shrill whistle desperately informing and alarming about Nana's arrival in [sd6] paralinguistically expresses the force of desperate alarm; the [sd7] proxemically displays the Neighbours' force of the ecstatic concentration in singing and dancing that stops all of a sudden as Nana arrives etc.

iii) Perlocutionary act

a) **Verbal Expressions:** The verbal responses in the turn taking at the *'Last letter starts the rhyme'* are the perlocutions of their earlier utterances, e.g. $u2$ to $u1$, $u6$ to $u5$, and $u8$ to $u7$ are the expected verbal perlocutionary responses observed here, since the rhymes are chained up by the *'Last letter'* as said in $sd1$, and as per the convention of the game.

b) **Non-verbal Expressions** (kinesic, paralinguistic, and proxemic): e.g. The sudden brake in the dancing and the singing (*'They all stop. A moment of total silence . . .'*) and the silence kinesically displayed in $sd6$, as soon as Nana arrives are the perlocutions to the desperate shrill whistle alarming about Nana's arrival. The shrill whistle itself is a paralinguistically expressed perlocution to the chaotic situation of the ecstatic singing and dancing of the Neighbours. The exit of all after Nana's, as mentioned in $sd9$ proxemically expresses the Neighbours' perlocution on Nana's leaving the place.

4.9 Sample-2 (act-2: p. 32-33)

The following sample has a speech situation that takes place at a crematorium. It shows the religious rite of offering rice-balls to crows, after the death of any family member. The two men performing the rite are engaged in a quarrel that questions the very purpose behind the rite.

(*sd1* *From the other side two men come out quarrelling. They are in their late thirties but both are dressed as little boys.*)

MAN 1: *u1* *You ought to be ashamed of yourself!*

MAN 2: *u2* *You watch your mouth.* (ibid. 32)

This is beginning of the quarrel. The stage direction sd1 informs about the queer dress and behavior of the characters. The queerness is felt due to the context of their age group.

MAN 1: *u3* *Shut up! Don't think to scare me! I am here with my father's rice-balls and nothing's going to scare me! And least of all, you. Seem to be new here. First death in the family? All going strong? If you don't know how to conduct yourself in a crematorium, you should bring some older person to show you.* (ibid…)

The above utterance informs about the rites and rituals to develop the socio-cultural context in which the rest of the situation is processed.

MAN 2: *u4* *I am all grown up! I don't need you to show me anything!*

MAN 1: *u5* *I see! Even your father wouldn't have offered the rice-balls this way!*

MAN 2: [u6] *You dare to mention my father! Poor, sainted soul!*

MAN1: [u7] *Oh! For someone who has just lost his father, you seem quite gay!*

The quarrel is intensified here. The situation shows a tug of war between the feelings and acts like the mechanical performance of the rituals, respect for the dead ones and cursing each other's fathers. This create stress in the situation.

MAN 2: [u8] *Watch your long wagging tongue, you!*

MAN 1: [u9] *Listen you! You come and put your balls right next to mine—[p1] I mean my father's—[p2] and on top of it you call me obscene names!*

MAN 2: [u10] *Obscene? Me?*

MAN 1: [u11] *That remark about my long tongue was decidedly obscene!*

The childlike dresses of these characters and their childish behavior complement each other. The discussion on what is obscene sounds absurd in this context.

MAN 2: [u12] *Nonsense! Nonsense! It was you who called me obscene names! And in my situation too! Here I am, a fatherless son offering his newly departed father's soul a pious offering and you call me 'gay'! I am a straight man, I am telling you!*

MAN 1: [u13] *This is absurd! I was referring to the expression on your face and the vigour of your speech.* (ibid 33)

MAN 1 and MAN 2 keep cursing and blaming each other. Their strange behavior contributes to the absurd element in this situation.

MAN 2: [u14] *My face? It is sad and anxious. I am awaiting the crow, my father's soul. If he is not hungry and does not peck at my balls, I will have to make one out of straw and my father's soul won't like that, I am sure.*

So stop chattering. Stop scaring the crow. (ibid…)

The situation concludes here showcasing the edge of blind beliefs over rationalism.

4.9.1 Sample 2: features and observations

• The sample has a single speech situation with only two characters
• A spotlight on the rituals followed after the death of any family member
• Explication of the individual's sorrow and the social satire
• The socio-religious influence on an individual's emotional world

4.9.2 Sample-2: analysis

1. **Addressers and Addressees**

   a) **Interpersonally operating**
   Man 1 and Man 2 (see [u1] to [u14]).

   b) **Ideationally operating**
   i) **Directly Ideational (directly from the author to the audience):**

The author-addresser addresses ([sd1]) the reader-addressees and the performer-addressees.

   ii) **Indirectly Ideational (indirectly from the author to the audience, through the characters):**

   The author-addresser addresses the reader-addressees and the performer-addressees through the characters' exchange of the utterances ([u1] to [u14]).

2. **Context**

   i) **Socio-cultural Dimension:**

   The beliefs in the society, e.g. the religious rites and the rituals in Hindu community, after the death of any family member, as it is observed in [u14] cited below:

> *'I am awaiting the crow, my father's soul.*
> *If he is not hungry and does not peck*
> *at my balls, I will have to make one out*
> *of straw and my father's soul won't like*
> *that, I am sure'.*

Finding

The socio-cultural reality of the rituals after death operates here as the context to the speech in this situation without which the perception of the speech would be difficult for all the addressees.

ii) Literary Dimension:

The literary convention of using the stage directions in drama (see [sd1] here) operates as the context to the present speech situation, since the details like the age, the dress, and the manner of the Men in conversation are shared through [sd1], with which the reader-addressees' and the performer-addressees' perception of the entire speech situation is facilitated.

The stage directions in drama, as a literary convention operate here as the context in the reader-addressees' and the performer-addressees' perception of the speech situation, the same in the other kinds of performances operate ideationally (through the performing-addressers' physical presentation of the age, the dress and the manner of the Men in conversation) as the context in the viewer-addressees' and the tele-viewer-addressees' and the audio-addressees' perception of the speech situation.

Finding

The stage directions in the print form operate as the context of the interpersonal communication between the author-addresser and the reader-addressees, and the performer-addressees, whereas the same in the non-print form operate as the context of the ideational communication between the author-addresser and the viewer-addressees, the tele-viewer-addressees, and the audio-addressees.

Hence, the context emerging from the stage directions operates through the different channels of transmission like the interpersonal and the ideational channel, depending upon the type of the performance.

iii) Theatrical Dimension:

This speech situation is processed in the context created by the use of the light effects and the stage property that are seen in the photograph (some other theatrical components can also form and operate as the context, however, the observations made here are on the basis of the facts found in the literary text and especially in the photograph, which is also part of the text, being produced in the script).

The use of lights, e.g. the use of spotlight on the two Men in quarrel highlights their verbal and non-verbal communication, and the area unnecessary for the same is faded away by darkening the rest of the stage. The theatrical convention of the use of the spotlight operates here as the context, since it plays as the shared background knowledge between the author-addresser (as the photograph is produced in the script), the performing addressers, the reader-addressees, the performer-addressees, and the viewer-addressees.

The use of stage property, e.g. the use of the spotlight assessed above, and also the use of the theatrical convention of using the level (covered with a black cloth,) also operates as the context of the communication between the author-addresser (as the photograph is produced in the script), the performing addressers, the reader-addressees, the performer-addressees, and the viewer-addressees.

Finding

The various theatrical conventions, being part of the shared knowledge of the various addressers and addressees, emerge as the context and operate as the 'contextualization cues' (Kramsch: 1998: 27) for the addressees in the speech situations in drama.

3. **Speech acts**

   i) **Locutionary act**

      a) **Phonetic act:** A primary stress is observed at the opening of the utterances, e.g. *'Shut up'* ([u3]), *'Watch'* ([u8]), *'Listen'* ([u9]), and *'Nonsense, nonsense'* ([u12]). The stresses look very obvious in the context of [sd1] that informs about the quarrel of the two Men.

      b) **Phatic act:** The use of the 24 exclamatory marks in the 14 utterances ([u1] to [u14]), although statistically may or may not bring out the type of locution, but the conventional meaning of the use of an exclamatory mark (that an exclamatory mark indicates the exclamation of some emotion), certainly determines the locution as an emotional exclamation of the quarrel.

c) **Rhetic act:** The use of *'Shut up'* ([u3]), *'Watch'* ([u8]), *'Listen'* ([u9]), *'Obscene'* ([u10]) and *'Nonsense, nonsense'* ([u12]) used at the very opening of the concerned utterances, rhetorically helps anticipating the tone of the quarrel, which is revealed in the rest of the utterance.

ii) Illocutionary act

a) **Verbal Forces:** e.g. The force of quarrel comes out through the repeated use of the terms of address *'you'* (used 16 times), *'your'* (used 6 times), and *'yourself'* (used twice), used to blame and call *'obscene names'* (see [u9] to [u12]) to each other by the two Men in this situation. The high frequency of the use of these terms of address brings out the force of quarrel in this situation.

b) **Non-verbal Forces** (kinesic, paralinguistic, and proxemic): e.g. The force of the quarrel operates kinesically, as referred to below:

MAN 1: [u13] *. . . I was referring to the expression on your face and the vigour of your speech.*

MAN 2: [u14] *My face? It is sad and anxious*

In [u7], the expression *'Oh! . . .'* paralinguistically expresses the force of Man 1's surprise and disbelief in, what Man 2 says earlier about his dead father.

MAN 2: [u6] *You dare to mention my father! Poor, sainted soul!*

MAN1: [u7] ***Oh!*** *For someone who has just lost his father, you seem quite gay!*)

The space distancing in [sd1] ([sd1] *From the other side two men come out quarrelling.*), <u>proxemically</u> contributes to the concerned addressees' perception of the force of quarrel.

iii) <u>Perlocutionary act</u>

   a) **Verbal Expressions:** e.g. In the context of the quarrel, the uncooperativeness, the impoliteness, the anger, and the warning observed in [u3] can be called a perlocution to the force of warning and anger in [u2].

MAN 2: [u2] *You watch your mouth.*

MAN 1: [u3] *Shut up! Don't think to scare me!*).

The perlocution in [u3] in turn, again operates as a locutionary act, which again executes the illocutionary force of warning and anger to arouse the perlocution of the strong disagreement in [u4].

MAN 2: [u4] *I am all grown up! I don't need you to show me anything!.*

Findings

1. **Both the illocutions and the perlocutions violate the cooperative principle and also the politeness principle.**
2. **The perlocutions again operate as the locutions and the illocutions, to cause new perlocutions, and the same recur cyclically throughout the situation.**

If the same perlocutionary act also operates here as a locutionary act and as an illocutionary act, it can be stated the same utterance operates all these three acts.

Hence, an utterance doesn't have any speech-act-specific identity, or the operational scope of any utterance is not restricted to any particular speech act, or the operational area of any utterance may not exactly coincide with the operational area of the speech act operating through it.

b) **Non-verbal Expressions** (kinesic, paralinguistic, and proxemic): e.g. The kinesic responses referred to in [u13], operate as a perlocution to [u12]

MAN 1: [u13] *This is absurd! I was referring to* **the expression on your face** *and the vigour of your speech.*

MAN 2: [u12] *Nonsense! Nonsense! . . . you call me 'gay'! I am a straight man, I am telling you!*

The <u>paralinguistic response</u> '*Oh!*' in [u7] is a perlocution showing disbelief and disagreement to the force of a son's (Man 2) intimate feelings expressed in [u6] for his dead father.

MAN 2: [u6] *You dare to mention my father! Poor, sainted soul!*

MAN1: [u7] *Oh! For someone who has just lost his father, you seem quite gay!*

No major finding of the <u>proxemic responses</u> is observed in this speech situation however, in [sd1] the <u>proxemic responses</u> given to each other by the two Men can be cited as some minor operations of this kind.

The analysis of the situations from *The Dread Departure* ends up here. The next part of this chapter analyzes the speech situations from the play *Evam Indrajit* by Badal Sircar (1989).

4.10 Evam Indrajit: analysis

Badal Sircar's *Evam Indrajit* gives certain insights into the modern life. The mechanical life of the modern bureaucrats is reflected well in the samples selected for the analysis. The play is summarized below.

4.11 About Evam Indrajit

Evam Indrajit written by Badal Sircar and translated into English by Girish Karnad is marked with the use of the absurdist note, the instrumental characters and the theme of identity crisis in it. The absurdist note is found in the features like meaninglessness, frustrations and mechanical life of the people in the play. The instrumental nature of the characters is observed in the multiple roles allotted to the same characters, as per the demand of the action. The theme of the identity crisis is found reflected in the very title of the play *'Evam Indrajit'*, which means 'and Indrajit' (here, 'and' denotes the insignificance of the very existence of Indrajit). The name Indrajit has a mythological context of victory of a demon over the god Indra. While the mythological Indrajit creates an indelible identity of his own, as a contradiction to the same, the modern Indrajit gets no identity of his own. Also the multiple roles allotted to the same characters, in a way, present the characters with no specific identity and thereby underline the theme of the identity crisis in the play.

The play opens with a Writer's desperate search for some theme to write his play. Auntie, the motherly figure is seen annoyed with his being too busy with the work of playwriting, which goes on, even at the cost of his food, rest and many other human needs. Manasi, the writer's own inspiration personified, suggests him some theme based on the everyday life of the people around him. The Writer initially finds the theme not very potent, but later on starts working with it. He calls some people (Amal, Vimal, Kamal and Indrajit) from the audience and begins to explore a play out of them.

Indrajit's adolescence, his love for Manasi and the social taboo attached to it (she is his first cousin on the mother's side), his realization of futility of that love, his visit to London resulting into his disappointment and a lot of such developments in the play bring out the theme of the absurdity of human existence. After knowing these experiences of Indrajit, though the Writer thinks there isn't the stuff he is looking for in Indrajit, still being insisted by Manasi, he continues his exploration of the play with Indrajit. Later on, Indrajit is shown married to a giggling wife; he addresses her also as Manasi and it is absurd. Finally, Indrajit's dreams of love and the ideas of his being extraordinary get ruined, and he is seen frustrated with the absurdity of his very existence as an ordinary person.

Badal Sircar uses certain dramatic gimmicks of placing Indrajit in his emotional past (by showing his one scene with real Manasi) and then taking him straight into a sort of limbo. The Writer, in the end, asserts his belief in the absurdity of the life, by describing it as an unending travel, futile, irrational and meaningless.

The note of absurdity, visited frequently through out the play, naturally influences the composition and the operation of the speech situations in the play. The speech situations from this play are assessed in the following part of the analysis.

4.12 Sample-1 (p. 5—6)

From *Three Modern Indian Plays* (1989), O.U.P.

In this sample a writer is seen in search of some theme to write his play on. The writer's being too busy with his writing annoys Auntie, the motherly figure. Being unable to find out any theme, when the writer feels vexed and tears the papers, Manasi, his inspiration personified, appears and helps him exploring the theme. The writer calls some people from the audience, so as to find and develop some theme out of their day-today living.

> ([sd1] *A table with a huge piles of papers on it. Sitting on the chair in front of it is the writer, his back to the audience. He is writing. Perhaps he has been writing for some time.*
> [sd2] *'Auntie' enters. She is called 'auntie' here only for convenience. She could be 'mother', 'elder sister', anything. She is frantic because she can't make any sense of her boy's behaviour. But then, not being able to make sense is the prerogative of 'aunties'.*) (ibid.5)

The stage directions sd1 and sd2 develop the context of this situation. A specific way of naming the characters as 'Writer' and 'Auntie' indicates that the characters' identity is not individualized deliberately. This is an important marker for the pragmatic analysis of the situation.

AUNTIE: [u1] *I just can't understand you!* (*[sd3] No response from the Writer.*) [p1]

I'm asking you . . . [p2] *are you coming in to eat or aren't you? You are the limit! I can't put up with this any longer . . .* (*[sd4] No response.*) [p3] *Why don't you speak?*

WRITER: [u2] *I'll have finished in a moment.* (ibid…)

The above utterances and the stage directions give some idea of the interpersonal relationship between these characters.

AUNTIE: [u3] *You have already said that three times—I am not going to call you again.*

WRITER: [u4] *You have said that three times too, Auntie.*

AUNTIE: [u5] *Do what you want. Night and day—scribble, scribble, scribble. No food, no drink, just scribble. Only God knows what will come out of all this scribbling . . . .* [p4] (ibid…)

The Writer writing and Auntie's comments on the same need be analyzed from the view point of what is implicated in these speech acts.

> ([sd5] *She goes out grumbling. The 'scribbling' has of course come to a stop already. The Writer gets up and walks downstage reading what he has written so far. A girl comes in. She will be called 'Manasi'.*)

MANASI: [u6] *Finished?*

WRITER: [u7] *No.* (ibid…)

The name 'Manasi' given above to this character is an important marker to study. Manasi's interest in the Writer's writing, as seen below also is a significant point, if compared with Auntie's reactions on the same.

MANASI: [u8] *Won't you read out what you have written so far?*

WRITER: [u9] *Haven't written a thing.* ([sd6] *Tears up the papers.*)

MANASI: [u10] *Why did you do that?*

WRITER: [u11] *It's no good. I have nothing to write about.*

MANASI: [u12] *Nothing?* (ibid…)

The utterances u8 to u12 bring out the interaction between Manasi and Writer showing concern of these characters regarding writing.

WRITER: [u13] *What shall I write? Who shall I write about? How many people do I know? And what do I know about them?*

MANASI: ([sd7] *Pointing to the audience.*) [u14] *There are all these people. Don't you know anything about any one of them?* (ibid...)

The above interaction shows that Manasi works as a manifestation of the Writer's inner mind. The Writer's search of 'theme' is on. It's clearly evident in the following citation.

WRITER: [u15] *Them? Oh yes. I d know a couple of them. A few like us. But they won't make a play.*

MANASI: [u16] *Try.*

WRITER: [u17] *I have tried.* (ibid. 6)

The attempts to find out a theme finally succeed, when the Writer happens to notice the 'four gentlemen' in the audience. The entry of the gentlemen is metaphorically indicated as clicking of an idea related to the theme the Writer has been looking for.

([sd8] *He throws away the bits of paper and goes back to the table. After a brief*

> *pause Manasi goes out. The Writer turns round suddenly and advances towards the audience. At exactly this moment four gentlemen are looking for their seats in the auditorium. The writer calls out to them.)*
> (ibid…)

The utterance u 18 below shows affection of the Writer towards his characters and the theme, he has been long waiting for. The politeness in the markers like 'listen, my dear, please, would you mind' brings out the force of request.

[u18] *Listen . . . . [p5] My dear sir . . . . [p6] You there . . . . [p7]*

FIRST MAN: [u19] *Eh! Are you addressing us?*

WRITER: [u20] *Yes, please. Would you mind stepping over here for a moment?*

SECOND: [u21] *All of us?*

THIRD: [u22] *On stage?*

WRITER: [u23] *Yes, if you don't mind. There's some important work.*

> ([sd9] *The four advance towards the stage.*)
> (ibid…)

The situation concludes with an indication that the Writer finds a germ to develop the script of his play. Apart from the observations noted above, the sample has some more features and observations as follows:

4.12.1 Sample-1: features and observations

- The sample contains one speech situation with three speech events (from ^{sd1} to ^{u5}; from ^{sd5} to ^{u17}; and from ^{sd8} to ^{sd9})
- The use of gimmicks (e.g. ^{u18}: the characters' participation invited from the audience)
- The features of absurdity, e.g. nothingness in ^{u11}, restlessness in $^{u9, sd6}$
- The variation of the techniques and the gimmicks in the characterization
- The use of the artifacts (e.g. the table, the chair and the papers) helping to establish the characters and the situation

---

4.12.2 Sample-1: analysis

1. Addressers and Addressees
a) Interpersonally operating

Auntie ($^{u1, u3}$ and ^{u5}); Writer (e.g. $^{u2, u7, u18}$ etc.); Manasi (e.g. $^{u6, u8, u16}$ etc.); First Man (^{u19}); Second (^{u21}); Third (^{u22}); Fourth (^{sd8} and ^{sd9}).

The interpersonally operating addressers and addressees mentioned above belong to different contexts and emerge as the different kinds of representation.

1. Auntie belongs to the context of minor characters, and represents the type of *'Aunties'* (see [sd2]).
2. Writer belongs to the context of the dramatic gimmick, 'play within a play', and represents the playwrights.
3. Manasi belongs to the context of the literary convention i.e., personification, and represents *'Manasi—the creation of Writer's mind'* and *perhaps an Indian counterpart of Jung's 'Anima"*, as Satyadeo Dubey describes it so in his introduction to this play (see *Three Modern Indian Plays*: 1989).
4. The Four Men belong to the context of the theatrical gimmick, the audience participating as the characters. They represent the masses, whereby the audiences and also the masses are directly connected with the performance of the play.

By and large, these characters bridge the different worlds like the literary world, the theatrical world and the societal world.

Findings

1. **The different contexts, to which the different addressers and addressees belong, operate as the connecting factors between the literary, the theatrical and the societal worlds.**

2. **The speech situations in drama can operate simultaneously at the multiple contextual levels of the different worlds.**

   b) **<u>Ideationally operating</u>**
      i) **Directly Ideational (directly from the author to the audience):**

The directly ideational address by the author-addresser (^{sd1} to ^{sd9}) is marked with the liberty offered to the addressees' 'say' (be they the reader-addressees or the performer-addressees) in the communication process of the play.

e.g. ^{sd2} *'Auntie' enters. She is called 'auntie' here only for convenience. She could be 'mother', 'elder sister', anything.'*

The choices of calling *'Auntie'* a *'mother',* an *'elder sister'* or *'anything'* like that, offer some liberty to the readers and the actors, to have their 'say' in the communication process of the play.

   ii) **Indirectly Ideational (indirectly from the author to the audience through the characters):**

The author-addresser addresses the reader-addressees and the performer-addressees through the characters' exchange of the utterances (^{u1} to ^{u23}).

For instance, the following utterances exchanged between the Writer and Manasi ideationally communicate the playwright's search of a play.

'WRITER: [u13] *What shall I write? Who shall I write about? How many people do I know? And what do I know about them?*

MANASI: ([sd7] *Pointing to the audience.*) [u14] *There are all these people. Don't you know anything about any one of them?'*

2. Context
i) Socio-cultural Dimension:

The socio-cultural dimension of the motherly affection for a son functions as the context, wherein the utterances [u1] to [u5]; and the stage directions [sd3] to [sd5] become meaningful.

The relationship between the Writer and Auntie is not only a typical Indian socio-cultural reality, but the same is found in the various cultures all over the world. In this sense, **the present point of socio-cultural context gets certain universal application.**

ii) Literary Dimension:

The use of the literary device personification, i.e. Manasi appearing as the Writer's inspiration personified, offers the literary dimension of the context to the utterances especially from [u6] to [u17].

The knowledge of the personification, as a device, functions as the shared background between the author-addresser and the addressees.

The catchy and the effective use of the personification and especially the 'surprise element' projected through it, takes the same very close to the status of the gimmicks used in drama. In this sense, **even gimmicks can operate certain contextual dimension, as the one discussed here.**

iii) Theatrical Dimension:

The theatrical dimension of the context is found operating in the use of the theatrical gimmick of calling the spectators from the auditorium (see [u18] to [sd9]) and thus inviting their participation in the performance.

The utterances, especially from [u18] to [u23], are processed in the context of this gimmick.

Finding

The gimmicks used in drama emerge as certain contextual dimensions in the process of the communication in drama.

3. Speech acts
i) <u>Locutionary act</u>
a) **Phonetic act:** The phonetic act is assessed with reference to the utterance ^{u1}. This utterance is divided by the pauses $_{p1, p2}$ and $_{p3}$, which cause rise of the tone in Auntie's voice after each division, as follows:.

AUNTIE: ^{u1} *I just can't understand you!*

(^{sd3} *No response from the Writer.*)$_{p1}$

I'm asking you . . . $_{p2}$ *are you coming in to eat or aren't you? You are the limit! I can't put up with this any longer . . .*

(^{sd4} *No response.*) $_{p3}$ *Why don't you speak?*

The 'no response' from the Writer causes irritation on the part of Auntie, and as an obvious result, it is assumable that her questioning, in particular, would phonetically execute a rising tone in her voice, after each pause of the Writer.

Here the pauses are found to be the cause of this specific development of the rising intonation.

<u>Findings</u>

The phonetic act is influenced by the pauses.

The pauses and the rising intonation are found in an alternate sequence in the execution of the phonetic act.

> b) **Phatic act:** The phatic act is analyzed here with reference to the question form of the utterances [u12] and [u13].

WRITER: [u11] *It's no good. I have nothing to write about.*

MANASI: [u12] *Nothing?*

WRITER: [u13] *What shall I write? Who shall I write about? How many people do I know? And what do I know about them?*

The phatic act found in the repeatedly used questioning pattern creates an illocutionary force of nothingness (the worry of '*nothing*' to be written). Thus, by creating the illocutionary force, **the phatic act proves to be complementary to the function of the illocutionary act.**

> c) **Rhetic act:** The rhetic act used in the following utterance is an operation of the rhetorical device of repetition, where the utterance '*scribble*' is used repeatedly.

AUNTIE: [u5] *Do what you want. Night and day—**scribble, scribble, scribble.** No food, no drink, just **scribble**. Only God knows what will come out of all this **scribbling** . . .* [p4]

The repetition of the utterance *'scribble'* brings out a force against the very act of *'scribbling'*. The force, brought out so, is an illocutionary force of apathy, transmitted against the Writer's being busy with writing.

Thus, by creating the illocutionary force, **the rhetic act proves to be complementary to the function of the illocutionary act.**

<u>Finding</u>

The rhetic and the phatic acts prove to be complementary to the function of the illocutionary act.

ii) <u>**Illocutionary act**</u>

a) **Verbal Forces:** The verbal force is analyzed here with reference to the utterances $u11, u12, u13$ and the utterance $u5$, which are already discussed under the analysis of the phatic act and the rhetic act respectively. The verbal forces, analyzed here, open up a very subtle aspect of the absurdity.

The verbal force that comes out of the utterances $u11, u12$ and $u13$ is the **force of nothingness** that there is nothing to write on, for the Writer.

And the verbal force that emerges out of the utterance u^5 is the **force of apathy** against the Writer's being too busy with writing.

The two forces mentioned above, if analyzed together, give rise to a chaotic and self-contradictory expression of the illocutionary **force of absurdity.**

The absurdity is the result of the contradiction that there is *'nothing'* to write and yet the writer is *'busy'* at the writing table.

The perception of the force of absurdity is facilitated verbally together by the complementary use of the phatic act (the questions emerging the force of nothingness) and the rhetic act (the repetition emerging the force of apathy) as discussed in details earlier.

Finding

The illocutionary force absurdity is brought out by the complementary operation of the phatic act and the rhetic act.

b) **Non-verbal Forces** (kinesic, paralinguistic, and proxemic): e.g. The non-verbal force of the Writer's restlessness is transmitted non-verbally. The transmission of the force of restlessness operates <u>kinesically</u> in ^{sd6}, through the Writer's action of *'tearing up the papers'*, and <u>proxemically</u> in [sd8], through his movements of restlessness (*'He throws away the bits of paper and goes back to the table.'*). The sample doesn't show the paralinguistic transmission of any force or message.

iii) <u>Perlocutionary act</u>

The perlocutionary acts transmitted both verbally and non-verbally are analyzed in the light of the following utterances.

WRITER: [u18] *Listen . . . . [p5] My dear sir . . . . [p6] You there . . . . [p7]*

FIRST MAN: [u19] *Eh! Are you addressing us?*

WRITER: [u20] *Yes, please. Would you mind stepping over here for a moment?*

SECOND: [u21] *All of us?*

THIRD: [u22] *On stage?*

WRITER: [u23] *Yes, if you don't mind. There's some important work.*

      ([sd9] *The four advance towards the stage.*)

a) **Verbal Expressions:** The verbally transmitted perlocutionary acts are [u19] as a perlocution to [u18], and [u21] and [u22] as perlocutions to [u20].

b) Non-verbal Expressions (kinesic, paralinguistic, and proxemic)**:**

The non-verbally transmitted perlocutionary act is [sd9], as a perlocution to [u18, u20] and [u23] expressed <u>proxemically,</u> through the space distancing of the 'four' heading towards the stage.

The perlocutionary act performed verbally and non-verbally here is an intermixed act of the 'four' spectators, initially (the verbal act of) confirming what they have heard, and eventually (the non-verbal act of) heading towards the stage, as a response or the perlocution to the act of the Writer's appeal to them to come on the stage.

The intermixed operation of the verbal and the non-verbal perlocutionary acts proves their function to be complementary to each other.

4.13 Sample-2 (p. 30—31)

From *Three Modern Indian Plays* (1989), O.U.P.

This sample shows an office and the mechanical bureaucratic life of the middle-class people working there. The Writer and his four characters: Amal, Vimal, Kamal and Indrajit perform the scene. The four characters perform as the employees in the office, whereas, the writer like a typical 'sutradhar', introduces the action and performs three different roles as the narrator or the Writer, as the Boss and as the Peon. The action begins as follows:

> (*[sd1]* *An office. Four chairs in a row. In another part of the stage, a big chair, a big table with a telephone on it. The writer is dusting the furniture—barely touching it with the duster.*) (ibid. 30)

The situation opens with the above stage direction projecting a typical office with stereotype markers of the physical context like 'the furniture', and of the psychological context like the person working without commitment.

> *WRITER:* (*[sd2]* *Coming downstage.*) *[u1]* *From home to school. From school to college. From college to the world. The world is an office. Like this one. A lot of business is transacted here—very important business. A lot of people work here—Amal, Vimal, Kamal and Indrajit.* (*[sd3]* *Amal and Vimal come in.*) (ibid…)

The utterance u1 brings out the lifeless routine of the office. In this context the 'important business' sounds an ironic comment. The names of the characters too seem to be a mere iconic representation of the stock characters.

> *AMAL:* *[u2]* *The 8.52 was ten minutes late today.*

> *VIMAL:* *[u3]* *A tram broke down near Sealdah station and there was a huge traffic jam.* (*[sd4]* *Kamal and Indrajit come in. Amal and Vimal sit down.*)

> *KAMAL:* *[u4]* *Today I missed the 9.13 again.* (ibid…)

'The 8.52' is a train-time used as a name. Kolkata setting is clearly evident, as the name of the place *'Sealdah station'* is mentioned.

INDRAJIT: [u5] *I had to let two buses go. There wasn't even enough space to hang on. (*[sd5] *Kamal and Indrajit sit down.)*

AMAL: (*[sd6] *To Vimal)* [u6] *How is your son?*

VIMAL: [u7]*Better.* (*[sd7] *To Kamal)* [u8]*Has your daughter secured admission?*

KAMAL: [u9] *No such luck.* (*[sd8] *To Indrajit)* [u10] *Have you found your pen?*

INDRAJIT: [u11] *No. Must have been stolen.* (ibid…)

It's a scene showing day-today chat of the office employees talking about everything except for their own business. The reference to 'the lost pen' can be taken as an indicator of their lost sense of duty.

AMAL: [u12] *Hareesh . . .*

VIMAL: [u13] *Hareesh . . .*

KAMAL: [u14] *Hareesh . . .*

INDRAJIT: [u15] *Hareesh . . .*

AMAL: (*[sd9] *A little more loudly.)* [u16] *Hareesh . . .*

WRITER: [u17] *Yes, Sir.* (ibid…)

The call out *'Hareesh… Hareesh…'* used repeatedly and the late reply to the same establish the numbness of the bureaucratic mentality.

AMAL: [u18] *Bring me a glass of water.*

VIMAL: ([sd10] *Loudly*). [u19] *Hareesh . . .*

WRITER: [u20] *Yes, Sir.*

VIMAL: [u21] *Bring me a betel-leaf and zarda.* (ibid…)

The above utterances bring out the officials' expectations from their subordinates that are more personal and less official. It continues in the following example too.

KAMAL: [u22] *Two cigarettes—'Scissors'!*

INDRAJIT: ([sd11]*Loudly*). [u23] *Hareesh . . .*

WRITER: [u24] *Yes, Sir.*

INDRAJIT: [u25] *Post this letter.* ([sd12] *The Writer doesn't move. Nor do they give him anything. They don't even look at him.*) (ibid. 31)

Experimental theatre stages the scenes like the one cited above. The action in this scene is suggestively left incomplete. The stock characters, the stock situation, the same actor playing various roles are some significant features of this scene.

AMAL: [u26] *The pick-pockets have become such a terrible nuisance. The other day when the Dharamtalla tram left the Mowlali stop . . .*

VIMAL: [u27] *If you want homoeopathic medicine see Kanai Bhattacharya. My brother-in-law had chronic dysentery . . . (ibid…)*

There are some more markers of Kolkata setting and the day today communication in the above example.

KAMAL: [u28] *They are giving her an admission test for the third standard. Can you imagine! English, Bengali and Arithmetic! On top of that they want the birth certificate.*

> *(*[sd13] *The Writer becomes the boss and strides in. The three half rise and then sit down scratching their heads. The writer takes his seat and the telephone rings.) (ibid…)*

The stage direction sd13 brings out the modern life, whereas u28 manifests the day today challenges before the modern man.

WRITER: [u29] *Hello—hello—yes—yes—order—invoice—delivery—fifteen per cent—yes—yes—bye. (*[sd14] *Changes files from the 'In' tray to the 'Out' and back again. Amal goes in and gets a file signed. Comes* *out. Then Vimal. Then Kamal. Then Indrajit. Then the phone.*) (ibid…)

The telephonic communication brings out modernity. The 'in' and 'out' trays also contribute to the same. The play has several examples which explicate the modern life and its problems. The following example is almost identical to the scenes discussed previously. Repetition of the scenes itself emerges as the signifier and the signified at the same time. It is repetition that brings out the boredom and the absurdity of the modern life.

WRITER: [u30] *Hello—hello—yes—yes—order—invoice—delivery—fifteen per cent—yes—yes—bye.* ([sd15] *Changes files from 'In' tray to 'Out'.*)

AMAL: [u31] *Hareesh . . .*

VIMAL: [u32] *Hareesh . . .*

KAMAL: [u33] *Hareesh . . .*

INDRAJIT: [u34] *Hareesh . . .*

> ([sd16] *The Writer moves to the peon's stool with the duster in his hand.* [sd17] Again the calls.) (ibid…)

The examples discussed above evolve many characteristic features. A few of them are produced in the following section.

4.13.1 Sample 2: features and observations

- The sample contains one speech situation with three speech events, from [sd1] to [sd12]; [u26] to [u28]; and [sd13] to [u33]).

- Absurdity in the modern life of middle class

- Repetition, a major device used with variations for the various functions

- Kolkatta setting (e.g. references in [u3], *'A tram'*, *'Sealdah station'* etc.)

- Broken & unidirectional communication (e.g. [u25] to [u28])

- Street-play treatment (e.g. change of the roles and the scenes, as seen in [sd13] and [sd16]; also in repetitions e.g. [u12] to [u15], and [u31] to [u34] etc.)

- Multiple roles of the same persons (e.g. the 'Writer' the 'Peon' and the 'Boss' played by the same person)

- The characters are representatives, yet they're not employed as the fixed signs for the fixed objects, but are placed in the varied contexts and in the various roles, what explicate the pragmatic dimensions, rather than the semiotic ones.

- The use of the artifacts to establish the identity of the roles (e.g. the stool and the duster for the Peon, and the chair, the table and the telephone for the Boss)

- The stage directions operate as the instructions to the actors, rather than the information to the readers.

4.13.2 Sample-2: analysis

1. Addressers and Addressees
a) Interpersonally operating

The Writer (^{u1}): also as Hareesh, the Peon (^{sd1} and ^{sd16}) and as the Boss (^{sd13});

Amal, Vimal, Kamal and Indrajit (as the people working in the office. See $^{sd3, sd4}$ and the various other stage directions and the utterances in which they interpersonally operate as the addressers and addressees.)

The present sample operates a very remarkable technique of the multiple roles of the same characters, played as per the convenience of the action. The technique focuses upon the theme of the identity crisis and also brings out the instrumental status of the characters.

Finding

The multiple addressers and addressees played by the same persons bring out:

1. **The theme of the identity crisis.**
2. **The instrumental status of the 'dramatis personae'** (Abrams: 1971: 124).

b) Ideationally operating
i) Directly Ideational (directly from the author to the audience):

The directly ideational address is assessed here, with reference to all the stage directions, where the author-addresser is found instructing to the actors, i.e. the performer-addressees, rather than informing the reader-addressees, about the action in the play. For instance, the stage direction [sd2], *'Coming downstage'* is explicitly more an instruction to the concerned actor, rather than an information to the readers.

However, what is communicated directly to the actors, is communicated indirectly to the readers as well. In this sense, the one and the same stage direction, while performs the perlocutionary function of persuading the performers to enact, also performs the locutionary function of informing to the reader-addressees about the same.

Finding

The same address of the author-addresser, directed to the two different addressees, operates two different speech acts, at the same time.

ii) Indirectly Ideational (indirectly from the author to the audience, through the characters):

The notion of the indirectly ideational address is highlighted in the present sample, by the technique of the multiple roles, allotted to the same performers.

The same performer delivers the various utterances, e.g. [u1] as the Writer, [u17] as the Peon, and [u29] as the Boss, to ideationally communicate the author's various messages, i.e. introducing the situation through [u1], bringing out the Peon's reluctance to work, by saying *'Yes, Sir'* through [u17, u20] and [u24], and focusing the mechanical communication of the 'Bosses' in such offices through [u29] and [u30].

By delivering the various utterances, the same performer hereby follows the various allotments on his part, made so by the author. This proves the instrumental status of the characters, and by the by also evolves the author as the main communicator, in this process of communication.

Thus, such a process of communication, while brings out the character's 'play', and communicates the author's 'say' to the audiences, operates therein as the

indirectly ideational address (i.e. the address indirectly from the author to the audience, through the characters).

Precisely, the notion of the indirectly ideational address is strongly supported in the present sample.

2. Context
i) Socio-cultural Dimension:

The socio-cultural dimension in the present situation is found operating as the middle class bureaucracy, in the Kolkatta setting. The situation opens with the scene of '*An office*' (see [sd1]) and the frequent references are made to the things and the places like '*the tram*', '*the Sealdah station*' in [u3], and '*the Dharamtalla tram*', '*the Mowlali stop*' in [u26].

The bureaucratic life in the Kolkatta setting offers the context to all the utterances in this speech situation.

The factors like the social class and its mentality, the place of action ('*office*') and the setting (Kolkatta) compose the socio-cultural context in this speech situation.

ii) Literary Dimension:

The literary dimension of the context is discussed in the light of the various features of absurdity, found in the present speech situation.

For instance, the utterances ^{u26} to ^{u28} project one literary feature of absurdity, i.e. the broken communication, in the context of which the second speech event (i.e. from ^{u26} to ^{u28}) in this speech situation is processed.

The problems like the broken communication, meaninglessness, nothingness and some other absurdities in the modern life come out as the various literary features of absurdity, as mentioned above.

The audiences' shared knowledge of such literary features attains the status of the context, which obviously facilitates their perception of the speech situation.

iii) Theatrical Dimension:

This speech situation is marked by the use of the artifacts (the stage property), which create certain ambience that helps to establish the identities of certain characters and certain speech events.

The use of the artifacts, (e.g. the stool and the duster used by the Peon in [sd1] and [sd16]; and the chair, the table and the telephone used by the Boss in [sd13]) creates the ambience, required to establish the two different identities of the same performer, as the Peon and as the Boss, in three different speech events that take place in the office.

These roles and the communication are perceivable in the context of the ambience, created by the use of the artifacts.

Finding

The use of the situation-specific stage property develops the situation-specific ambience, to develop the theatrical context of that speech situation.

3. **Speech acts**
   i) **Locutionary act**

   The three types of locutionary speech act are discussed with the help of the various utterances as follows:.

   The phonetic act is discussed in the light of the monotony of the utterances [u12] to [u15], and [u31] to [u34].

The phatic act is analyzed with [u29] and [u30], which appear in an identical syntactic and compositional form.

The rhetic act is assessed with the help of the rhetorical devices used for the effective narration in [u1].

a) **Phonetic act:** The utterances [u12] to [u15]; and [u31] to [u34] have identical form of composition as follows:.

AMAL: [u12] *Hareesh . . .*

VIMAL: [u13] *Hareesh . . .*

KAMAL: [u14] *Hareesh . . .*

INDRAJIT: [u15] *Hareesh . . .*

These are the calls given repeatedly to the same person. The repetition is an expression of the monotony in the calls.

The compositional monotony can arouse the phonetic monotony too; and the compositional monotony is the author's act that helps the characters' act of executing the phonetic monotony.

b) **Phatic act:** The utterances [u29] and [u30] are composed in the following structural form.

*'WRITER: Hello—hello—yes—yes—order—invoice
—delivery—fifteen per cent—yes—yes—bye.'*

The act of saying operates here in the form of certain repeatedly used words in the repeatedly used structures.

The repetition brings out the monotonous communication in the monotonous life of the middle-class bureaucrats.

Briefly, **the use of the structural monotony is the real-life monotony expressed so; and using the structural monotony is the author's act that helps the characters' act of expressing the real-life monotony.**

c) Rhetic act:

The act of performing [u1] is the performance of a rhetic act, as it employs a literary and rhetorical device of repetition for the effective narration. The Writer-narrator introduces the speech situation as follows::

'WRITER: ([sd2] *Coming downstage.*) [u1] *From home to school. From school to college. From college to the world. The world is an office. Like this one. A lot of business is* transacted here—*very important business. A lot of people work here—Amal, Vimal, Kamal and Indrajit.'*

This utterance opens with three identical structures and also ends with two sentences identically structured that make the narration rhythmic and effective.

Briefly, the use of certain rhetorical devices (repeatedly used identical structures) makes the act of narration effective.

The act of using the rhetorical devices is the author's act that helps the character's act of the effective narration.

It is observed here that the three subtypes of the locutionary speech act operate the device of repetition, which is the author's non-speech act that helps the performance of the characters' locutionary speech act. In this sense, the characters' interpersonal locutionary speech acts come out of the author's ideational 'non-speech acts' (Leech: 1983: 214) of saying the same.

<u>Findings</u>

1. **The repetition emerges as the major device to perform the locutionary speech act.**
2. **The playwright's non-speech acts evolve the characters' locutionary speech acts.**

ii) <u>Illocutionary act</u>

   a) **Verbal Forces:** e.g. The force of an order comes out verbally in the utterances [u18, u19, u21,] and [u22] produced below.

AMAL: [u18] *Bring me a glass of water.*

VIMAL: ([sd10] *Loudly*). [u19] *Hareesh . . .*

WRITER: [u20] *Yes, Sir.*

VIMAL: [u21] *Bring me a betel-leaf and zarda.*

KAMAL: [u22] *Two cigarettes—'Scissors'!*

The utterances [u18] and [u21] are the imperative sentences expressing commands, in [u19] a peon is summoned by a *'loud'* call, whereas again in [u22] the peon is ordered. The relationship between the addressers (Vimal and Kamal) and the addressee (the Writer playing the role of Harish, the Peon) helps to understand the verbal force of the commands operating in the delivery of these utterances.

The relationship of the addressers and the addressee here operates as a determining factor in the operation of the force.

Finding

The relationship between the addressers and the addressees can determine the operation of the verbal illocutionary force.

b) **Non-verbal Forces** (kinesic, paralinguistic, and proxemic): The non-verbal illocutionary forces are discussed here with the functioning of the proxemic and the kinesic forces, operating in [sd13, sd14] and [sd15].

The sample doesn't show any significant operation of the paralinguistic transmission of the non-verbal forces.

The stage direction sd13 brings out the force of the powers of the Boss, transmitted proxemiclly, through his act of the space distancing, i.e. his way of walking, the 'striding in' the office.

The stage directions sd14 and sd15 bring out a kinesically transmitted force of the mechanical routine of the middle-class bureaucrats, as operates in the repeatedly mentioned action of 'Changing files from the 'In' tray to the 'Out' and back again'.

As far as the force of the mechanical routine of the bureaucratic life is concerned, the use of repetition, as a device, plays a determining role to transmit the force.

The device of repetition operates kinesically in a theatrical performance, and rhetorically in the literary performance.

Findings

1. **The kinesic transmission of the force in a theatrical performance operates as a counterpart to the rhetorical transmission of the same in the literary performance.**
2. **The mode of the transmission of the non-verbal forces varies, as the type of performance varies.**

iii) Perlocutionary act

a) **Verbal Expressions:** e.g. The utterance [u17] operates as the verbal expression of the perlocution, delivered in response to the utterances [u12, u13, u14, u15] and [u16].

AMAL: [u12] *Hareesh . . .*

VIMAL: [u13] *Hareesh . . .*

KAMAL: [u14] *Hareesh . . .*

INDRAJIT: [u15] *Hareesh . . .*

AMAL: ([sd9] *A little more loudly.*) [u16] *Hareesh . . .*

WRITER: [u17] *Yes, Sir.*

The calls given to Harish are responded to by saying *'Yes, Sir'* in [u17]. It is very clear that the perlocution in [u17] is a little long awaited and anticipated perlocution, and it is delivered as a common and collective response to the same call given by four different addressers.

Thus, the perlocution in [u17] operates as the single and collective perlocution to the same locution and the illocution delivered repeatedly by the different addressers.

Finding

The same and single verbal response operates as a collective perlocution to the same but multiple locutions and illocutions transmitted by the multiple addressers.

b) **Non-verbal Expressions** (kinesic, paralinguistic, and proxemic)**:** The sample doesn't show any significant operations of the paralinguistic and proxemic expressions of perlocution. The non-verbal expression of perlocution is discussed here with an example of a kinesic expression that operates in [sd13], as follows::

'The Writer becomes the boss and strides in. ***The three half rise and then sit down scratching their heads.****'*

The kinesically transmitted response of the *'half rising and siting down scratching their heads'*, by the *'three'*, operates as a mechanically expressed routine perlocution, to an equally mechanical and routine entry of the Boss in the office.

Here, the characters' 'being mechanical' is the author's illocution projected through the characters' non-verbal expression of the perlocution. Thus, the non-verbal perlocutionary act of the characters evolves out of the author's illocutionary non-speech act.

Finding

The playwright's illocution in his non-speech act evolves the characters' non-verbal perlocutionary act.

The analysis in this chapter closes with the above sample. The next chapter also deals with the analysis of the speech situations selected from the two plays, *Ghashiram Kotwal* (Tendulkar: 2000) and *Seven Steps Around The Fire* (Dattani: 2000).

4.14 Conclusion

This chapter thoroughly analyzes the speech situations from three plays. The analysis evolves a number of findings, which are generalized in the chapter of Conclusions. It is mainly observed that the operational mechanism of the speech situations changes, as the form of drama changes. It is also observed that the speech situations in the print form of drama are influenced by the components from the non-print form of drama as well.

The next chapter analyzes the samples selected from the remaining two plays, using the same analytical model.

CHAPTER-5

ANALYSIS

Playwriting . . . is a highly technical medium . . . , where you have to adhere to certain technical demands and function within limitations . . . you have to adjust to specific situations . . . visualize three dimensionally . . .

I can't think of the play as a literary activity in solitude. I must constantly test how it will sound, how it will look, where it will be staged . . . . Unless you live with the theatre you cannot write a satisfactory play.

(Tendulkar V. in Bhalla N. ed., 2000: 119-20)

5.1 Preliminaries

The present chapter includes the analysis of the speech situations from two different plays, Vijay Tendulkar's *Ghashiram Kotwal* (Tendulkar, 1986) and Mahesh Dattani's *Seven Steps Around the Fire* (Dattani, 1999).

Although, the analysis in this chapter also follows the same parameters, as used in the previous chapter of analysis, it attempts to bring out the various aspects of the speech situations that remain unexplored hitherto.

The speech situations, especially from the radio play, *Seven Steps Around the Fire,* throw light on the different aspects than those analyzed in the previous chapter. The analysis also attempts to explore all the samples with a view to the 'technical demands and function within limitations' (Tendulkar, 2000: 119). The limitations, influencing the process of playwriting, influence the operation of the speech situations and obviously also the analysis of the same.

While analyzing the playwright's 'say', the analysis doesn't ignore the performers' 'play' in it. However, since the data to be analyzed is in a literary form, the analysis of the performers' 'play' comparatively faces more 'limitations', which are due to what Stanislavski calls in his *Creating A Role* the 'complex patterns of creative emotions' (Stanislavski, 1981: 66). With regard to the performers' play, he writes:

> *First one must plot a line along which the passion will develop; one must comprehend, feel the component parts of the passion; one must prepare a whole scheme which will be like a canvas on which creative emotions will*

> *embroider consciously or unconsciously*
> *their inscrutable and complex patterns.*
> (Stanislavski, 1981:66)

On the one hand, playwriting, according to Tendulkar, is not merely a literary activity in solitude, but is a process three-dimensionally visualized for its theatrical expression, and on the other hand, a process to theatrically express the complex patterns of creative emotions, according to Stanislavski, is also not merely a theatrical business but needs the 'whole scheme' obviously including the 'literary activity' that normally precedes the theatrical expression.

Precisely, the literary and the theatrical expressions of the play in general and the speech situations in particular are interdependent, and so need be analyzed with a holistic approach. Hence, the holistic analytical view applied in the previous chapter—to analyze the playwright, the performers and the audiences (readers, viewers, listeners etc.) in the same analytical model together, as the addressers and the addressees in the literary, in the theatrical and in the socio-cultural contexts—continues in the present chapter too.

The analysis begins with the speech situations from Vijay Tendulkar's *Ghashiram Kotwal* (Tendulkar, 1986).

5.2 Ghashiram Kotwal: analysis

The present play is a milestone in the history of Marathi theatre. The speech situations in this play operate in the socio-historical context of *Peshwai*—the Peshawa regime. As per the form of analysis used in the thesis, two samples from this play are selected for the analysis. The plot of the play is summarized below, in order to facilitate the analysis.

5.3 About Ghashiram Kotwal

Ghashiram Kotwal (Tendulkar, 2003) like Tendulkar's other plays, *Gidhade* (Tendulkar: 1970), *Sakharam Binder* (Tendulkar, 1972) and so on, is a revolutionary work. The play is controversial, taking the theme, set in the historical context of the *Peshwai*. It highlights the corrupt practices during the period. However, Tendulkar (1999) denies calling the play, as a historical play. According to him, 'This is not a historical play. It is a story in verse, music and dance, set in a historical era.' (Tendulkar, 1999: 02)

The play brings out the degeneration and the moral and political corruption through the story of Ghashiram Kotwal, who was an official of Nana Phadanvis, the Peshawa's deputy in Pune, between 1769 and 1800. A folk-theatre tradition of *'nandi'* opens the plot of the power-politics rotating around Nana and Ghashiram. The play attacks the pleasure-seeking activities of the Brahmins from

Pune pampered at the cost of the comfort and the security of the toiling masses. Ghashiram, who is victimized by the ruling Brahmins, decides to take revenge upon them, and succeeds in getting appointed, as the city magistrate of Pune by Nana, the chief minister of the Peshawas. Ghashiram starts exerting his powers to take revenge upon the Brahmins brutally, and Nana ignores the same only because he exploits Ghashiram's daughter sexually and wants to continue it. With this, the brutality of Ghashiram's revenge is intensified and he tries to direct it to Nana also, but Nana maneuvers all his political skills, to trap Ghashiram and kill him publicly in the end.

The play on the one hand evolves and later also dismantles Nana, as an icon of the moral and the political corruption during the *Peshawai*, and on the other hand portrays Ghashiram, as the tragic hero of the play.

5.4 Sample-1 (act I: p. 361-2)

From *Collected Plays in Translation* by Vijay Tendulkar (2003)

The sample-1 is a *'nandi'*, with which the play opens. *'Sutradhar'* introduces the action and the characters in the play, in a typical tradition of the folk theatre, as follows:

> (*[sd1]* *Twelve men standing in a line, sing. Ganapati comes in.*)

ALL: ([sd2] *swaying to and fro*).
   [u1] *Ganapati dances the Ganapati dance,*
   Brahmans of Poona bow and prance. ([sd3]*Repeat.*)
   (ibid…)

The above part is a beautiful blending of dance and drama, as also of the mythological and socio-historical context. The scene continues below:

   … Pious Brahmans,
   Keep on dancing,
   Holy Ganapati,
   Keep on dancing. (ibid…)

Drama and poetry too are blended skillfully here. There is a striking parallelism between Brahmans and god Ganapati in their being ('pious and holy') and acting ('dancing').

   … Now let the drum beat!
   Now let the drama heat!
   Heaven, hell and earth complete!
   Heaven, hell and earth complete! (ibid…)

The poetic and musical strength of *'nandi'* is clearly evident in the above part.

   Saraswati-devi,
   Goddess of wisdom.

   ([sd4] *Saraswati enters dancing. Ganapati*
   and Saraswati dance.)

[u2] *Goddess of wisdom,* (ibid…)

The reference to gods creates mythological context in which the utterances become meaningful.

… Wife of the Great One.
Shri Ganaraya,
Image of good luck,
Even the mountains
Bow to your name. (ibid…)

God Ganaraya is praised in a traditional manner of the folk play here.

Play, Saraswati,
Goddess of music.
Come Lakshmi-devi,
Wife of the Great One, (ibid…)

Gods are invited through such prayers; and in a way, the morale of the performers is boosted.

… Bow to the good God.
Both of you dance.

> *([sd5] Lakshmi comes in and dances with the two.)* (ibid…)

The dance of the gods and goddesses is a typical feature of the folk tradition. Some special costumes and masks are used to perform these roles.

[u3] *Shri Ganaraya,*

Now you must bless us.
*All that we ask for—*_{p1}
Success for this play! (ibid…)

The very purpose of this prayer *'Success for this play'* is revealed in the above part. The performers have to maintain their morale high during the performance. Their psychological strength is earned from the mythological and the socio-cultural context in which they live.

*Blessed image—*_{p2} *morya!*
*Ganapati bappa—*_{p3} *morya!*
Blessed image
Ganapati bappa! (ibid. 362)

'Morya' is not just another name of god Ganapati. When chanted loudly in a chorus, it's a source to energize folks.

> (^{sd6} *This is repeated. The tempo increases.*
> *It ends with 'mor . . . ya'!*
> *Ganapati, Lakshmi and Saraswati go off*
> *stage.*)

^{u4} *Blesser of Pundalik, Hari, Viththal,*
Dnyanadev, Tukaram.

In the above utterance, *'Pundalik, Hari, Viththal, Dnyanadev, Tukaram'* is a remarkable religious slogan that is deeply rooted in the socio-cultural fabric of Maharashtra state in India. This is yet another source to energize folks.

(ˢᵈ⁷ *Again, slower, deeper, rhythmically*)

ᵘ⁵ *Ganapati dances the Ganapati dance.*

We the Poona Brahmans bow and prance.

We the pious Brahmans bow and prance. (ibid…)

The repetition of the above lines enhances the musical quality of this prayer.

SUTRADHAR: (ˢᵈ⁸ *saying 'Ho Ho' to all, stops the singing*).
ᵘ⁶ *These are all Brahmans from Poona.* ᵘ⁷ *Who are you?*

ONE MAN: ᵘ⁸*A Vedantic scholar.*

SUTRADHAR: ᵘ⁹ *You?*

SECOND: ᵘ¹⁰ *A Vaidya doctor.* (ibid…)

Sutradhar takes charge of the performance after the prayer and the action in the play continues with an introduction of the major and minor characters.

THIRD: ᵘ¹¹ *A logician.*

FOURTH: ᵘ¹² *An astrologer.*

FIFTH: ᵘ¹³ *A linguist.*

SIXTH: ᵘ¹⁴ *I am a baron.* (ibid…)

After the names are introduced, the places to which the characters belong are also introduced.

OTHERS: [u15] *I come from Shringeri.* [u16] *I come from Tanjore.*

> [u17] *I come from Rameshwar.* [u18] *I come from Kumbhakonam.*

> [u19] *I come from Banaras.* [u20] *We are Poona people.*

SUTRADHAR: [u21] *Good Good Good!* (ibid…)

The scene concludes with the introduction of the characters. Some more features and observations related to this sample are produced below:

5.4.1 Sample 1: features and observations

- The opening scene of the play
- The sample with one speech situation and two speech events ([sd1] to [u5;] and [sd8 to u21])
- The use of the *'Nandi'* and the *'Sutradhar'*, as the typical conventions in the Indian theatre
- The versified utterances
- The various contextual dimensions (socio-cultural, religious, theatrical etc.)
- The same characters in different roles, as the chorus and as the individuals

5.4.2 Sample-1: analysis

1. **Addressers and Addressees**

   a) **Interpersonally operating**

   Twelve Men (see [sd1]); Ganapati, Saraswati, Lakshmi (see [sd1, sd4, sd5]); Sutradhar[1] (see [u6]); One Man, Second, Third, Fourth, Fifth, Sixth, Others (see [u8] to [u20]).

   b) **Ideationally operating**

   i) **Directly Ideational (directly from the author to the audience):**

   The author-addresser addresses ([sd1] to [sd8]) the reader-addressees and the performer-addressees.

   ii) **Indirectly Ideational (indirectly from the author to the audience, through the characters):** The author-addresser addresses the reader-addressees and the performer-addressees through the characters' exchange of the utterances ([u1] to [u21]).

2. Context

i) Socio-cultural Dimension:

The socio-cultural dimension of the context operates in the form of the pantheistic, rather than the theistic socio-religious beliefs, e.g. the personification of gods and goddesses, and their presentation, as an intermixed existence with the human world (see [sd1, sd2, sd4, sd5,] and [sd6]). These beliefs or the shared knowledge of the beliefs operate here, as the context of the communication between all the addressers and addressees. (These beliefs may or may not be of the author addresser's own beliefs, yet his shared knowledge of these beliefs works as the context.)

ii) Literary Dimension:

The use of the Indian literary convention of worshipping gods and goddesses for the success of the play operates here, as the literary dimension of the context, which facilitates the addressees' perception of the situation. It is seen in [u3] as follows: *'Shri Ganaraya, Now you must bless us. All that we ask for—Success for this play!'* Also, the shared knowledge of the literary technique of allotting varied roles to the same character (e.g. characters playing chorus as well as some other roles here) operates as another literary dimension of the context.

iii) Theatrical Dimension:

The present speech situation is a *Nandi*[2], an Indian theatrical convention of invocation to gods and goddesses, for the success of the play, e.g. *'All that we ask for—Success for this play!'*

The Oxford Companion to Indian Theatre (Anandlal: 2004) illustrates *Nandi* as:

The essential ingredient of the purvaranga[3] *or preliminaries in Sanskrit theatre and later traditional forms. If the other elements of purvaranga are difficult to perform, the sutradhara must take special care that at least the nandi occurs before the actual play commences, as a means to remove any obstacles. The nandi designates whatever is recited in praise of a deity, Brahman, king, or the like, combined with a benediction . . . . and consists either of eight or twelve* **padas**[4] *(poetic lines). The sutradhara or* **sthapaka**[5] *(director) normally delivers it.* (Tripathi K. D. in Anandlal: 2004: 301)

The present sample shows all the features of the *nandi* mentioned in the above reference, e.g. the performance of the *nandi* before the actual play commences; the *Sutradhar* and his role, as described earlier; and the *'padas'*: the 'eight lines' (see $u3$) and 'twelve lines' (see $u1$ and $u2$).

Thus, the speech in this situation is processed in the context of the Indian theatrical conventions.

3. Speech acts

i) Locutionary act

a) **Phonetic act:** The phonetic execution of the utterance *'morya'* following $p2$ and $p3$ in $u3$, and also mentioned in $sd6$ has a typical Indian way of execution. The utterance is executed with a loud and long stretch of *'mor'* followed by *'ya'*, and it is often executed like a slogan by the chorus in the praise of god Ganapati.

b) **Phatic act:** As the phatic act of saying something is represented grammatically, the dashes indicating the pauses: $p1,$ $p2,$ and $p3$ operate as the locutionary acts, since conventionally the pauses express, what is unexpressed verbally.

Finding The phatic locution (the use of the grammar i.e. the punctuation marks: the dashes) is hereby found to be a non-verbal locution.

    c) **Rhetic act:** The versified utterances (^{u1} to ^{u5}) operate as the rhetic acts of the worship, and thereby rhetorically bring out the act of a typical Indian convention of offering prayers to gods, by means of singing.

ii) <u>Illocutionary act</u>

    a) **Verbal Forces:** e.g. The verbal force of the prayer comes out through the rhyme (e.g. the rhyme scheme of ^{u1}: a-a, b-c, d-c, e-e, f-f, g-h), the rhythm, and the repetition (^{sd3}), which are basically the literary devices, used as the acts in delivering the force of the prayer. In a theatrical performance, the verbal force in these literary devices comes out phonetically through varied intonation patterns. And so, a radio performance and a tele-visual performance and such other performance types can have their own operational mode in the delivery of the verbal force.

<u>Finding</u> **The verbal force has a literary mode of operation in the literary text, and the same in a theatrical performance is complemented with a phonetic mode of operation.**

So, the verbal force has a performance-specific operational mode, or the operational mode

of the verbal force varies, as the type of the performance varies.

b) **Non-verbal Forces** (kinesic, paralinguistic, and proxemic): e.g. The non-verbal force of the humble bowing in the prayer <u>kinesically</u> operates through the posture of a *namaskar*, an Indian convention used in the act of worshipping or welcoming (see the photograph). Sutradhar's saying: *'Ho Ho'* in [sd8], <u>paralinguistically</u> operates as the non-verbal force of concluding the prayer. [*SUTRADHAR:* (*[sd8] saying 'Ho Ho' to all, stops the singing)*]. The utterance *'Ho Ho'* is again an Indian conventional utterance normally used to stop anything (here, the singing). In [sd2] the non-verbal force of the dancing and prancing in the prayer is found to be a <u>proxemic</u> operation, as all the performing addressers in this situation make use of the space distancing [*ALL:* (*[sd2] swaying to and fro)*] in the delivery of the force.

The proxemic operation of the non-verbal force (see [sd2] above) is very much complementary to the verbal force of *'prancing'* (see [u1]) in the prayer. According to the Cambridge Advanced Learner's Dictionary (Woodford & Jackson: 2003), the meaning of *'prancing'* is as follows:

Prance / *verb*

1   I + adverb or preposition] to walk in an
     energetic way and with more movement
     than necessary: *It's pathetic to see*
     fifty-year-old rock stars prancing **around**
     on stage as if they were still teenagers.
     She pranced into the office and demanded
     to speak to the manager.
2   [I] When a horse prances it takes small,
     quick steps and raises its legs higher than
     usual.

As per the entry in the dictionary, the '*swaying to*
and fro' (the proxemic operation) mentioned in [sd2],
is found to be 'the energetic movement (prancing)'
of the quick steps in dancing. Thus the non-verbal
force operating proxemically in 'dancing' proves to
be complementary to the verbal force in 'prancing'.

Finding

**The non-verbal force operating proxemically
(here, in '*dancing*') proves to be
complementary to the verbal force (here, in
'*prancing*').**

iii) Perlocutionary act

a)   **Verbal Expressions:** e.g. The utterances:
     [u8] and [u10] to [u20] operate as the verbal
     expressions of the perlocution delivered

in response to the Sutradhar's utterance, [u7] '*Who are you?*'. The utterance [u7] is an introduction of the characters to the audience by the Sutradhar, through whose utterance operates a dramatic convention of introducing characters through other characters. Naturally, as the convention goes, the expected action in response to [u7] from the characters is their self introduction, which takes place through [u8] and through [u10] to [u20].

There are in all twelve varied verbal expressions ([u8] and [u10] to [u20]) that come out as the perlocutions i.e. the acts of self-introduction as a response to the same and only utterance [u7].

Finding

Single utterance can arouse multiple verbal responses.

However, though there are twelve varied verbal expressions ([u8] and [u10] to [u20], operating as the perlocutions), the function of the perlocutionary act performed by each is the same i.e. the act of self introduction.

Finding

Multiple verbal responses can perform the same and single perlocutionary act.

The two findings mentioned above evolve a new finding as follows:

Finding

The same and single utterance arousing the same and single perlocutionary act processes through multiple verbal expressions.

b) **Non-verbal Expressions** (kinesic, paralinguistic, and proxemic): e.g. The <u>kinesic response</u> of Saraswati (mentioned in [sd4]: *'Saraswati enters dancing. Ganapati and Saraswati dance'*); and the same of Lakshmi (mentioned in [sd5]: *Lakshmi comes in and dances with the two.*) operate as the perlocutions to the dance of Ganapati and All (see [sd2, sd3] and [u1]).

No major <u>paralinguistic responses</u> are observed operating in this speech situation.

By leaving the stage, the characters of Ganapati, Saraswati and Lakshmi deliver their <u>proxemic response</u> to the last repetition of the utterance: *'mor . . . ya!'* as mentioned in [sd6]: *(This is repeated. The tempo increases. It ends with 'mor . . . ya'!*

Ganapati, Lakshmi and Saraswati go off stage.).

The last repetition of the utterance *'mor . . . ya!'* operates as a marker of the exit of these characters; and accordingly the characters respond to the same.

These responses operate by the proxemic act (the space distancing) of the characters that *'go off stage'*.

5.5 Sample-2 (act II: p. 414-6)

From *Collected Plays in Translation* by Vijay Tendulkar (2003)

The sample-2 is about the tragic end of Ghashiram and his powers. The political failure of Ghashiram is posed against Nana's political success of wrapping up Ghashiram's powers with his life.

SUTRADHAR: [u1] *And in the end came The End. (*[sd1] *Ghashiram, one hand tied behind his back, comes on stage. He has been beaten. Disfigured. Bloodied.)* [u2] *Ghashiram was thrown in front of the Brahmans with one hand tied behind his back. (*[sd2] *The Brahman line crouches like hunters. Once in a while they give a shout or mime an action such as throwing stones.)* (ibid. 414)

Every utterance is supported by stage directions. The narrative in the utterances and the action in the stage directions complement each other.

GHASHIRAM: [u3] *Hit me. Beat me. Beat me some more. Hit me!* ([sd3] *Suddenly Ghashiram shields his face as if a stone hit him.*) [u4] *Why stay so far away? Come on, you cowards. Still scared? I spit on you. Beat me. Come on, beat me. Come on and beat me. I dare you. Hit me. Look—one of my hands is tied. And you're scared! Come on, beat me. Crush me!* ([sd4] *The mob yells.*) (ibid…)

Ghashiram's emergence as a tragic hero is evident here in this play. The violence in this drama is a significant factor. It reaches its peak in the present scene.

[u5] *Ghashiram Savaldas! Ghashiram Savaldas! I danced on your chests but I wasted the life of my little daughter. I should be punished for the death of my daughter. Beat me. Beat me. Hit me. Cut off my hands and feet. Crack my skull. Come on, come on. Look! I'm here. Oh, that's good. Very good.* (ibid. 415)

Reference to Ghashiram's daughter in the play arouses feeling of pity. Cruelty and brutality of the human world stun the spectators.

([sd5] *The mob shouts. The drums beat loud and fast. Ghashiram begins to move in a sort of dance as if dying to the beat of the drum. Falls, gets up, falls, growls like an animal. Crawls. Jerks in spasms. Falls and falls again while trying to rise. Death dance. The crowd's shouting continues.* (ibid…)

Music and dance play an important role in this situation. It is the association of the different art forms that makes this play a composite art form. The above citation clearly brings out the same.

Finally Ghashiram lies motionless. Nana enters in a palanquin with the chief minister's pomp. Royal clothing. Gets down from the palanquin and raises one hand to calm the crowd.) (ibid…)

The death of Ghashiram sounds tragic at the backdrop of Nana's political moves. The misery of Ghashiram's death and the pomp of Nana's entry are paradoxical to each other. It is this paradox that communicates the situations effectively to the audience.

NANA: [u6] *Ladies and gentlemen. Citizens of Poona. A threat to the great city of Poona has been ended today. (*[sd6] *The crowd cheers) A disease has been controlled. The demon Ghashya Kotwal, who plagued all of us, has met his death. Everything has happened according to the wishes of the gods. The mercy of the gods is with us always.* (ibid…)

The play shows certain events in which the political moves are convinced to the crowd in the name of gods. The cunningness of the rulers and the madness of the mob remain hidden in the politically created garb of gods.

([sd7] *He nudges the corpse of Ghashiram with his walking stick.)* [u7] *Let the corpse of sinful Ghashya rot.*

> *Let the wolves and dogs have it. Let the worms have it. Whoever attempts to take away this corpse will be punished. Whoever mourns for him will be hanged. All living relatives of Ghashya Savaldas will be found, bound, and expelled from the city.*

The cruelty continues even after the death of Ghashiram. The idea of harassing his relatives proves the same.

> *We have ordered that from this day forward, not a word, not a stone relating to the sinner shall survive. We have commanded that there be festivities for three days to mark this happy occasion. (*[sd8] *The crowd shouts. Cheers. The line forms. Cymbals. Red powder. Festivity. Now Gulabi comes in dancing. Nana's wives come dancing. The crowd dances.)*
> (ibid. 416)

The idea of celebration showcases the worst face of brutality under the mask of so called justice.

> *ALL TOGETHER:* [u8] *Ganapati dances the Ganapati dance.*
> *Brahmans of Poona bow and prance.*
> *Now sound the drum beat!*
> *Now let the drama heat!*
> *Heaven, hell and earth—complete!*
> *Shri Ganaraya . . .* (ibid…)

The situation concludes here with the features and observations produced below:

5.5.1 Sample 2: features and observations

- The concluding scene from the play
- The use of the typical Indian dramatic and theatrical conventions
- The communication influenced with the theme of 'the power clash and the power shift'
- No two characters directly talk to each other
- The characters appearing as the group characters (e.g. *Crowd, Brahman line, All Together etc.*) & the individual characters
- The crowd as a group character in the non-verbal communication
- The madness of the mob

5.5.2 Sample-2: analysis

1. Addressers and Addressees

a) Interpersonally operating

Sutradhar ([u1] and [u2]); Ghashiram ([u3, u4, u5] and [sd1, sd3, sd5, sd7]); Nana ([u6, u7] and [sd7]); All Together ([u8]); Gulabi ([sd8]); The Brahman Line ([sd2]); The mob / The crowd ([sd4, sd5, sd6,] and [sd8]); Wives of Nana ([sd8]).

'All Together' in [u8] collectively operates as an independent character, so it is treated as an interpersonally operating (singular) addresser.

'The Brahman Line' ([sd2]) and *'Wives of Nana'* ([sd8]) also operate as the independent characters, so they too are distinctively treated as the interpersonally operating (singular) addressers.

However, on the basis of the context (the shared knowledge) of a theatrical convention that the same actors can play multiple roles, and also on the basis of the [sd4, sd5, sd6,] and [sd8], it seems possible that *'The Brahman Line'* and *'Wives of Nana'* can play also as the part of *'The mob / The crowd'*. In such a case of the same actors playing the varied roles, the analysis evolves the following finding.

Finding

The same performing addresser (actor) can play as more than one interpersonally operating addresser and addressee.

b) **Ideationally operating**

i) **Directly Ideational (directly from the author to the audience):**

The author-addresser addresses (^{sd1} to ^{sd8}) the reader-addressees and the performer-addressees.

The author-addresser's address, through his ideational narration (the message transfer through the narration) in ^{sd2}, facilitates the following.

1. he reader-addressees' perception of the illocutionary force of the attack (*The Brahman line crouches like hunters. Once in a while they give a shout or mime an action such as throwing stones.*).

2. The performer-addressees' i.e. the actors' perception and also the expression of the same illocutionary force of the attack.

ii) Indirectly Ideational (indirectly from the author to the audience, through the characters): The author-addresser addresses the reader-addressees and the performer-addressees through the characters' exchange of the utterances (^{u1} to ^{u8}).

For instance, the message transferred through *Sutradhar,* i.e. the indirectly ideational address of the author-addresser in ^{u1}:*'And in the end came The End.'* is a piece of the author-addresser's information to the audience, about the end of the play as well as the end of Ghashiram and his powers.

2. Context

i) Socio-cultural Dimension:

The socio-cultural convention of the celebration following the victory of the good over the evil operates here as the socio-cultural dimension of the context, in which the action in ^{sd8} is processed.

(*The crowd shouts. Cheers. The line forms. Cymbals. Red powder. Festivity. Now Gulabi comes in dancing. Nana's wives come dancing. The crowd dances.*)

Although, from the crowd's point of view, the celebration following the death of Ghashiram falls in line with the socio-cultural convention, but from a rational point of view, the manifestation of the very notions: the good (Nana and the crowd) and the evil (Ghashiram) are questionable here, since, Nana and the crowd don't seem to be 'that good', and Ghashiram doesn't seem to be 'that evil'.

So, when the very logic behind the crowd's celebration is questionable, the celebration proves to be absurd.

Thus, the crowd's mistaken application of the socio-cultural convention brings out an absurd manifestation of the same.

Finding

If a situation has some fuzzy logic operating at the contextual level, the action processed in it results into an absurd manifestation of the same.

ii) Literary Dimension:

The use of the chorus in [u8] is a literary convention, wherein the roles of all the characters get merged in the role of '*ALL TOGETHER*'. The message of the summing up of the situation is anticipated, due to the very conventional action of the merging of all the characters into the chorus. So, the very formation of the chorus, which is a contextual aspect here, communicates the conclusion of the situation earlier than the actual utterance (u^8) does the same. In this sense, the contextual aspect of u^8 influences the present speech situation more than the utterance itself.

The utterance u^8 is composed of the verbal (the song sequence) as well as the non-verbal communication (the dance sequence), which are also the operational aspects of the context of the chorus. In this sense, the context of the chorus engulfs and processes u^8, especially the verbal communication in u^8 in such a way that it mainly hints at the conclusion of the situation, rather than giving merely the verbal message of the prayer.

Precisely, the contextual aspect of u^8 influences the present speech situation more than (especially the verbal communication in u^8) the utterance itself does.

Although, the influence of the context is comparatively assessed here against the verbal aspect of the utterance, both the context and the utterance are complementary to each other in the overall communication of the speech situation.

Finding

In certain situations, the influences of certain components—like the context and the utterance—on the process of message communication are complementary with each other and at the same time also comparable.

iii) Theatrical Dimension:

An amalgam of music and acting creates the theatrical context of the death dance in [sd5]: *'The drums beat loud and fast. Ghashiram begins to move in a sort of dance as if dying to the beat of the drum.'*

The message of Ghashiram's death is effectively communicated in the theatrical context of the music and the acting.

3. Speech acts

i) Locutionary act

a) **Phonetic act:** The phonetic act is assessed with reference to the utterance [u6]: *'NANA: Ladies and gentlemen. Citizens of Poona. A threat to the great city of Poona has been ended today.* ([sd6]

The crowd cheers)'. As it is a beginning of the chief minister's address to the citizens, its phonetic execution sounds very typical.

The phonetic execution of the 'beginning of the address', observes a primary stress obviously placed on the utterances *'Ladies', 'gentlemen'* and *'Poona'*. The operation of the phonetic act in the present example is influenced by the custom of delivering the opening of a speech or an address, with the primary stresses as mentioned above, and also with the loud exclamation of the topic sentence: *'A threat to the great city of Poona has been ended today.'*, followed by *'The crowd's cheering'*.

However, in case of the other utterances, the operational mode of the phonetic execution will not be always influenced by such customs, but also by the factors like the actors' (performing addressers') choice of dialogue delivery.

b) **Phatic act:** The phatic act is analyzed here with reference to the use of the four short, imperative and repetitive sentences in [u3]: *'GHASHIRAM: Hit me. Beat me. Beat me some more. Hit me!'*. All the four sentences being short, imperative and repetitive, display a dominant conversational feature, which is the essence of drama. The use of the specific grammatical structures, bringing out the conversational feature, falls in line with Leech's 'complementarist view', on grammar and pragmatics, 'within an overall programme for studying language as a communication system' (Leech: 1983: X).

Finding

The phatic act facilitates the effective communication and therefore the former is pragmatically complementary to the latter.

c) **Rhetic act:** The utterances [u6] and [u7] emerge the chief minister Nana's character, as a rhetorician addressing his rhetoric effectively and persuasively to the Citizens. These utterances operate as the rhetic acts of addressing a speech to the said audience.

ii) Illocutionary act

a) **Verbal Forces:** e.g. The verbal force of the wrath of Ghashiram, exerted against the Crowd in [u3, u4] and [u5], and also against himself especially in [u5] are analyzed here. In expressing the verbal force of his anger, Ghashiram repeatedly uses the terms like '*hit, beat, spit, crush, crack,* *cut off, cowards, scared, dare, come on'* etc. Each of these terms communicates the 'sense' of the anger independently, whereas they communicate the 'force' of anger, when used repeatedly and perceived collectively.

Finding

The verbal 'sense' gets transformed into the verbal 'force', when certain verbal expressions are used repeatedly and perceived collectively.

b) **Non-verbal Forces** (kinesic, paralinguistic, and proxemic): e.g. The non-verbal force of the Crowd's ecstatic cheer comes out kinesically, paralinguistically and proxemically, due to the repeatedly and collectively transmitted actions in [sd4, sd5, sd6] and [sd8].

The actions of Crowd are transmitted as '*The mob yells* ([sd4]), *The mob shouts* ([sd5]), *The crowd's shouting continues* ([sd5]), *The crowd cheers* ([sd6]), *The crowd shouts. Cheers* ([sd8]), *The crowd dances* ([sd8])' etc.

Once again, it is observed that each of these non-verbal actions communicates the 'sense' of the cheer independently, whereas they communicate the ecstatic 'force' of the cheer when used repeatedly and collectively.

Finding

The non-verbal 'sense' gets transformed into the non-verbal 'force', when certain non-verbal actions are used repeatedly and perceived collectively.

iii) Perlocutionary act

The perlocutionary acts transmitted both verbally and non-verbally are analyzed in the light of the opening utterance of the present speech situation.

'SUTRADHAR: [u1] *And in the end came The End'.*

The utterance [u1] delivered by the Sutradhar arouses varied perlocutionary acts from Ghashiram, Nana and All together including the Sutradhar himself, with a changed role in the chorus.

Verbal Expressions: The verbally transmitted perlocutionary acts are [u3, u4, u5,] by Ghashiram, [u6, u7] by Nana and [u8] by All together. All these are the verbal expressions of the varied perlocutions to the same utterance [u1] mentioned above. By performing [u3, u4, u5,] Ghashiram meets '*The End*' of his reign and life; by performing [u6] and [u7], Nana brings about '*The End*' of Ghashiram's powers; whereas, by performing [u8], All together showcase '*The End*' of the play.

Thus, '*The End*' in Sutradhar's utterance [u1]: '*And in the end came The End.*' clearly hints at—'performing for audience'—the end of Ghashiram's life and powers, as well as the end of the play. As the response or the perlocution to the same hint, all the characters perform '*The End*', by performing their own perlocutionary acts varied from each others'. It is noteworthy here that the characters' varied perlocutionary acts 'of their own' are in fact not of their own, but are the pre-planned parts, in the overall decorum of the play. Thus, the operation of the characters' perlocutionary acts in particular, and the speech situation in general, is influenced here by the factor of performing or showing to the audience, which is a typical feature of the speech situations in drama.

Findings

1. The characters' perlocutionary acts 'of their own' are in fact not of their own, but are the pre-planned parts in the overall decorum of the play.
2. The operation of the speech situations in general and the speech acts in particular is influenced by the factor of performing or

showcasing, for the audience, as per the scheme of performance.

3. **The act of performing for the audience emerges as an instrumental act of the performance.**

In the light of the finding no. 1, and as compared with the perlocutionary acts, **the case is different with the illocutionary acts,** which allow greater scope to the individuality of the actors or the performing addressers, as they can take some liberty 'in saying' (Austin: 1962) or in performing their acts.

Precisely, the illocutionary acts are not so much pre-planned parts of the overall decorum of the play, as much the perlocutionary acts are.

c) **Non-verbal Expressions** (kinesic, paralinguistic, and proxemic):

The responses of the *Brahman line* to bring about *'The End'* of Ghashiram's life and powers, as mentioned in [sd2], are the non-verbal expressions, which are performed kinesically, paralinguistically and proxemically, as perlocutions to the [u1]: *'And in the end came The End.'*

It is observed as follows:: *'The Brahman line crouches like hunters* (<u>proxemic response</u>).

> *Once in a while they give a shout* (<u>paralinguistic response</u>) *or mime* (<u>kinesic response</u>) *an action such as throwing stones.'*

Not only the *Brahman line*, but also the *Crowd, Gulabi, Nana's Wives* and *All Together*, perform the varied perlocutionary acts, by using the varied non-verbal expressions in response to [u1], so as to bring about either *'The End'* of Ghashiram's life and powers, or *'The End'* of the play.

The analysis of the speech situations from *Ghashiram Kotwal* (Tendulkar: 1986) concludes hereby. The next play to be analyzed is Mahesh Dattani's *Seven Steps Around The Fire* (Dattani: 2000). The following section introduces the analysis of the selected speech situations from this play.

5.6 Seven Steps Around The Fire: analysis

The present play, being a radio play, has very different kind of speech situations, as compared to those studied earlier. The speech situations are phonetically dominant in this play. The samples selected for the analysis display certain medium-specific features of the radio plays.

5.7 About Seven Steps Around The Fire

The radio play, *Seven Steps Around The Fire* by Mahesh Dattani is characterized with the typical radio-play features like the use of sounds, silences, pauses, voice-over etc. The playwright sets the play in a stark reality of the socio-cultural ethos in the contemporary world. The play candidly uncovers the problems of the gender identity of the *hijra* community, their sexual exploitation and social isolation. The storyline of the play is developed, as the investigation of the murder mystery of a *hijra* person, who is married by the son of a minister.

A flashback opens the play, with a hint of some marriage situation, immediately followed by a scream of a dying person. The whole play develops in the context of the same flashbacked situation, and progresses to unveil the murder mystery, which after getting unveiled is veiled again, once and for all.

Subbu, the son of the minister Mr. Sharma falls in love with the *hijra* person named Kamla. Despite the domestic and the social objections they get married; however, soon Kamla is brutally burnt alive by the men of the minister. The case is hushed up. Later on, Uma the protagonist—who is a researcher in sociology, wife of Mr. Suresh, the police superintendent, and daughter of the vice chancellor of a University—investigates the same case, as a part of her thesis. She succeeds to uncover the case with the help of a police constable named Munswamy and some *hijra* persons like Anarkali and Champa. However, when she shares the result of her investigation with Suresh, he and his senior authority take every measure to hush up the case once again and forever.

Uma's 'voice-over' used in the end of the play sums up the total episode with an exasperating note on the bitter and brutal reality.

The picture of such a dark and stark reality obviously influences all the speech situations in this play. A few of such situations are produced for the analysis in the following samples:

5.8 Sample-1 (p. 7)

From *Collected Plays* by Mahesh Dattani (2000)

The sample opens the action with a flashback ([sd1] below) that hints at Subbu's wedding with Kamla, followed by Kamla's murder. After the flashback, begins the main action, wherein Uma starts her investigation of Kamla's murder case. Munswamy, the constable helps her in it. The scene place as follows:

> [sd1] ([u1]*Sanskrit mantras fade in, the ones chanted during a Hindu wedding. Fire. The sound of the fire grows louder,*

drowning the mantras. [u2] *A scream. The flames engulf the scream.*) (ibid…)

This is a very special kind of scene which has a stage direction containing two utterances. Normally the utterances are in the dialogue form, but here they are part of a stage direction. Since the 'mantras' are chanted and the 'scream' is a shout, they are treated here as utterances. The following scene takes place in the office of the police superintendent.

[sd2]Interior. The office of the superintendent of police.

([sd3]*Whirring of fan* ([sd4]*stays throughout the scene). Rustle of paper. Footsteps approaching.*)

MUNSWAMY: [u3] *You may see the hijra now if you wish, madam.* (ibid…)

Uma comes to meet Kamla. Munswamy ushers her in to the prisoner.

UMA: [u4] *Will she talk to me?*

MUNSWAMY: ([sd5]*chuckling*). [u5] *She! Of course it will talk to you. We will beat it up if it doesn't.* ([sd6]*Rustle of paper. Pause* $_{p1}$.) (ibid…)

Munswamy's 'chuckling' indicates that he ridicules the question. Ridiculing Uma's question is ridiculing Kamla's existence itself. The use of pronouns 'she' by Uma and 'it' by Munswamy for the same person bring out the difference of their attitudes to look at the eunuchs.

[u6] *Madam, if you don't mind me saying, why is a lady from a respectable family like yourself . . . . [p2]?There are so many other cases. All murder cases. Man killing wife, wife killing man's lover, brother killing brother. And that shelf is full of dowry death cases. Shall I ask the peon to dust all these files?* (ibid…)

This is Munswamy's talk to Uma. According to him, a lady like Uma should not spoil her status by involving in the case like Kamla's. However, Uma remains firm on her stand.

UMA: [u7] *No. Maybe some other time. I think this particular one is of interest to me at this time.*

MUNSWAMY: [u8] *If you don't mind me saying, what is the use of talking with it? It will only tell you lies. I will bring it.*

UMA: [u9] *No. Can I meet her in there?* ([sd7] *Prison gates clang shut.*)

This situation concludes here. the clanging of the prisoner gate and the other sounds are markers of the nonverbal communication in this radio drama. The following section throws light on some more features and observations relevant to radio plays.

5.8.1 Sample 1: features and observations

- The sample has two different speech situations from the radio-play
- The first situation (see ^{sd1}) is a flashbacked situation, in the context of which the whole action of the play gets processed
- The flashback is an entire speech situation transmitted by only one stage direction (^{sd1})
- The second situation (^{sd2} to ^{u7}) commences the actual action in the play
- The Typical radio-play directions perform the various functions e.g.

  The ^{sd1} brings out the flashback and thereby the entire speech situation

  The ^{sd2} establishes the place of action

  The $^{sd3, sd4, sd5, sd6}$ and ^{sd7} inform about the various sounds used for the various functions
- The typical radio-play utterances, e.g. the phonetically dominant utterances centered on, what Bharatmuni calls '*vachik abhinaya*' (*Natyashtra*: chapter no. 17, see Anandlal: 2004)

5.8.2 Sample-1: analysis

1. Addressers and Addressees

a) Interpersonally operating

Munswamy ($^{u3, u5, u6, u8}$ and ^{sd5}) and Uma ($^{u4, u7}$ and ^{u9}).

The interpersonal exchange of communication between these two characters brings out the two distinct points of view, operating in the same situation. The distinct points of view bring out the two distinct attitudes towards *'hijras'*, the eunuchs. These attitudes come out from the two distinct pronouns, used as the terms of address for the *hijra*, as seen in the following exchange of the utterances.

UMA: [u4] *Will* **she** *talk to me?*

MUNSWAMY: ([sd5]*chuckling*). [u5] *She! Of course* **it** *will talk to you. We will beat it up if it doesn't.*

The pronouns *'she'* and *'it'* used for the *hijra* by Uma and Munswamy, respectively reflect Uma's humane attitude of respect, and Munswamy's inhuman attitude of disregard, towards the *hijra* community. As far as the gender identity and the gender respect are concerned, in the Indian cultural setup, Uma's term of address *'she'* is more polite and respectful than Munswamy's used term of address *'it'.* This is what Ashok Thorat (2006) says precisely, *'The point here is that politeness here is context-specific and communicator-dependent phenomenon'.* (Thorat: 2006: 131)

The terms of address used by the characters in the interpersonal communication, to address a character not present in person in the situation, influence the overall process of drawing inferences from the speech situation.

Finding

1. **The use of the different terms of address, by the different addressers, for the same addressee, facilitates the perception of the different points of view, operating the different attitudes, in the same situation.**

Precisely, the inferences on the attitudes of the addressers and addressees are influenced by the use of the terms of address.

b) Ideationally operating

i) Directly Ideational (directly from the author to the audience):

The sample shows an entire speech situation (transmitted as the flashback in ^{sd1}), communicated ideationally by the author-addresser to the audiences.

By using only one stage direction—which marks the precision of the communication in terms of space—and by using the technique of the flashback—which marks the precision of the communication in terms of time—the author-addresser here transmits one complete and centrally significant speech situation, around which this radio play rotates.

The dramatic medium of the stage direction and the dramatic convention of the flashback, both causing their respective precisions, satisfy the demand of the compactness of the radio performance.

Thus, the demand of the compactness here determines:

i)   The compactness of the space in the stage direction [sd1], which subsequently determines the compact composition of the speech situation in it.

ii) The compactness of the time in the flashback, which subsequently determines the compact transmission of the speech situation.

The compactness is a medium-specific demand here, in a sense that the very demand is determined by the strengths and weaknesses of the medium e.g. the time limit set for the radio performances.

Finding

The radio plays have certain medium-specific strengths and weaknesses, which influence the author-addresser's ideational communication and thereby determine both the composition and the transmission of the speech situations.

ii) **Indirectly Ideational (indirectly from the author to the audience, through the characters):**

The author-addresser addresses the reader-addressees, the performer-addressees and the radio-addressees indirectly through the characters' exchange of the utterances ($u1$ to $u9$).

For instance, in the radio performance, the author-addresser's message transferred through $u1$ i.e. the *'Sanskrit mantras fading in'*, hinting at some marriage; and also the message transferred through $u2$ i.e. *'A scream'* hinting at some mishap, are the indirectly ideational addresses, since in the radio performance, the utterances $u1$ and $u2$ are supposed to be performed indirectly by the playwright through the actors' phonetic transmission of the same.

However, in the literary performance, from where the present sample is collected, the same utterances $u1$ and $u2$

operate as parts of the stage direction [sd1], which, as a whole address, is not an indirectly ideational address, but a directly ideational address, since in the literary performance, the author-addresser directly transmits the message in [u1] and [u2] himself by means of his narration.

So, the performing addressers', i.e. the actors' phonetic transmission of the utterances [u1] and [u2] in the radio performance, and the author-addresser's narration of the same in the literary performance, categorize the use of the same utterances differently, depending upon the two different types of performances, as an indirectly ideational addresses in the radio performance, and as the directly ideational address in the literary performance.

Thus, the address that is indirectly ideational in the radio performance becomes directly ideational in the literary performance.

Finding

The same address undergoes the varied modes of transmission, depending upon the varied types of performances.

2. Context

i) Socio-cultural Dimension:

The socio-cultural dimension of the context operates here in the socio-cultural identity and the status offered to the *'hijra'* community. At the backdrop of the socio-culturally pejorative identity and the lowly status of the *'hijras'*, the following utterances, especially the expressions highlighted and underlined, become meaningful.

UMA: [u4] *Will **she** talk to me?*

MUNSWAMY: ([sd5]**chuckling**). [u5] ***She!** Of course **it** will talk to you. We will **beat it** up if **it** doesn't.* ([sd6] *Rustle of paper. Pause* [p1].) [u6] **Madam**, *if you don't mind me saying, why is **a lady** from **a respectable family** like yourself . . . .* [p2]*?*

Two examples of contrast bring it out vividly:

a) The contrast between the educated and cultured Uma's use of the respectful term of address '***she***' for the *hijra*, and Munswamy's use of the regardless term of address '***it***', voicing the malign mediocre mentality towards the same person.

b) The contrast between Munswamy's chuckling, as a reaction to the respectful identity offered to the *'hijra'* by Uma, and Munswamy's use of terms like Madam and lady for Uma, who according to him belongs to a respectable family.

Thus, the socio-cultural identity and the status of the *'hijra'* community operate as the context, in which the above utterances and the whole situation are meaningfully processed.

ii) Literary Dimension:

The literary dimension of the context operates in the use of a typical radio-play direction:

[sd2] **'Interior. The office of the superintendent of police.'**

The direction appears as a literary convention and as per the convention informs about the place of action, so as to offer the background knowledge, which is essential to process and make meaningful the speech and the whole situation following it.

The direction [sd2] works as the literary context of the situation.

iii) Theatrical Dimension:

The flashback in [sd1] emerges as the theatrical dimension of the context, since the next situation and the action throughout the play get processed in it.

The flashback: *'Fire. The sound of the fire grows louder, drowning the mantras. A scream. The flames engulf the scream.'*, sets the background or the context of the speech situation that takes place at *'the office of the superintendent of police'*, as mentioned in [sd2]. The theatrical technique of the flashback that operates here as the context to the next situation, itself is a speech situation in the background.

Thus, the speech situation in the flashback offers context to the speech situation following it. In fact, the whole performance of the play takes place in the context of this particular situation flashbacked here. When the play rotates around any situation like this, the speech situation emerges as **a pivotal situation** that offers context to not only a few other situations in the play but to the whole play.

Finding

In drama, there can be any pivotal situation that offers context to some other speech situations in the play and the whole action of the play.

3. Speech acts

i) Locutionary act

a) **Phonetic act:** The phonetic act is discussed here with reference to the utterance [u2]: '*A scream. The flames engulf the scream.*'

In the present literary performance, the act of '*screaming*' is one of the most important acts. The whole play is about the '*scream*' and '*engulfing the scream.*' of the *hijra* community. In this sense, this is an act 'of saying' (Austin: 1962:120) a lot metaphorically without saying much phonetically.

In the radio performance, the phonetic execution of the '*screaming*' is initially supposed to operate at a high pitch and later muffled by the sound of the flames. The execution of the phonetic act in the radio performance is an execution of the paralinguistic sound of screaming, accompanied by the musical sound of flames. Both the paralinguistic sound and the musical sound jointly compose and transmit this locutionary phonetic speech act in the radio performance.

Precisely, the metaphorical 'act of saying' in the literary performance emerges as the counterpart of the joint paralinguistic and musical 'acts of saying' in the radio performance.

Thus, the locutionary phonetic act here shows some medium—specific distinct modes 'of saying' the same.

Finding

The locutionary phonetic act has some medium—specific distinct modes 'of saying' the same.

b) **Phatic act:** The phatic act is analyzed here with reference to the pause $_{p2}$ used by Munswamy as follows::

'Madam, if you don't mind me saying, why is a lady from a respectable family like yourself . . . . $_{p2}$?'

The act of pausing can be inferred on the basis of Munswamy's attitudes towards *'hijras'* and towards Uma, manifested throughout the sample, as the act of saying: *'Madam . . . why is a lady from a respectable family like yourself* **should at all involve in the cases of 'hijras'**?'

The highlighted part is the verbal counterpart of the act of pausing, inferred so. On the basis of the inference drawn here, the phatic act of pausing is an 'act of saying' nothing phonetically, and yet it's an 'act of saying' a lot metaphorically through the grammatical device of the dots used for the act of pausing.

Finding

The phatic 'act of saying' something metaphorically and non-verbally can be traced out of an 'act of saying' nothing phonetically and verbally.

c) **Rhetic act:** The use of the rhetic act is discussed here with an example of the utterance [u1]: *'Sanskrit mantras fade in, the ones chanted during a Hindu wedding.'* The *'Sanskrit mantras'* referred to have certain conventional meaning, which is derivable even semantically, since the *'mantras'* are full of semantically derivable 'sense' (Leech: 1983: 30). The semantic sense of the rhetic 'act of saying' or *'chanting'* the *'mantras',* as per its denotations and connotations, communicates the proceedings of a marriage situation.

Not the semantic sense only, but even the pragmatic 'force' (Leech: 1983: 30) of the rhetic 'act of saying' or *'chanting'* the *'mantras'*—which although in the further process of the pragmatic exploration can evolve various implicatures—basically projects the proceedings of the marriage situation.

By and large, on exploring the present rhetic act, to a certain length of the exploration, it is found that certain pragmatic dimensions of the rhetic act coincide with its semantic dimensions.

Finding

The coinciding of the semantic and the pragmatic dimensions of the rhetic act is traceable to a certain length of exploration.

ii) **Illocutionary act**

The illocutionary act is assessed here with reference to the verbal and the non-verbal forces of the offence hinting at the lowly gender identity of the *hijra* community in the Indian socio-cultural context.

a) **Verbal Forces:** e.g. The word *hijra* used in [u3] projects a pejorative force of the malign mediocre mentality in the Indian socio-cultural context, hinting at the lowly gender identity offered to the community of the persons, referred to so. The utterance belongs to the Indian languages and here appears as a mixed code, which is a deliberate usage, since the pragmatic scope of the force transmitted through this Indian utterance, and that of its counterparts from English language like 'eunuch' or 'impotent', do not coincide, as the intensity of the offence in the use of the Indian utterance is comparatively far greater, and so not derivable from its English counterparts.

Precisely, the code mixing of the utterance *hijra* is necessary to bring out the right intensity of the offence caused by the usage of the utterance in the Indian cultural context.

Finding

The intensity of the verbal force is language specific, since the interpretation of language is culture-specific.

b) **Non-verbal Forces** (kinesic, paralinguistic, and proxemic): e.g. The same pejorative force of offence non-verbally emerges out of Munswamy's chuckling, as seen in [sd5] below:

UMA: [u4] *Will she talk to me?*

MUNSWAMY: ([sd5]***chuckling***).[u5] *She! Of course it will talk to you.*

The non-verbal force is a paralinguistic manifestation of the force exerted through the specific kind of laughing at the *hijra* community.

iii) **Perlocutionary act**

a) **Verbal Expressions:** The verbally performed perlocutionary act is discussed with reference to the following exchange of the utterances.

UMA: [u4] *Will she talk to me?*

MUNSWAMY: ([sd5]*chuckling*). [u5] *She! Of course it will talk to you. We will beat it up if it doesn't.*

The verbal response [u5] is perlocutionary to the utterance [u4]. In fact, [u4] is a yes/no type of question and so it expects some perlocution like yes or no. However, the perlocution in [u5] is different and far more than the expected one. Munswamy's sarcastic expression of the views on the gender identity is something uncalled for, along with his 'yes' type of response, which is called for.

The perlocutions in [u5] come out in the two forms, as an expected response and an unexpected response.

The unexpected response has the force of sarcasm that comes out independently, with no connectivity with Uma's question.

In exerting the force of the unexpected response, this particular part of the perlocution performs an illocutionary function. So, the perlocutionary act is found to perform the illocutionary act also.

Finding

The perlocutionary acts also can perform illocutionary functions.

> **b) Non-verbal Expressions** (kinesic, paralinguistic, and proxemic)**:**
>
> The radio plays have their own strengths and limitations, and as far as the non-verbal expressions are concerned, the radio plays display their strength of operating the paralinguistic expressions, and also the limitations in displaying the kinesic and the proxemic responses.
>
> The paralinguistic response of chuckling in ^{sd5} operates as a perlocution to ^{u4}. Besides this, the sample shows a few other non-verbal expressions of the

pauses ($_{p1}$ and $_{p2}$) that operate as the non-verbal perlocutionary acts in the following example.

(^{sd6}*Rustle of paper. Pause* $_{p1}$.)

^{u6} *Madam, if you don't mind me saying, why is a lady from a respectable family like yourself . . . .* $_{p2}$?

As seen in the sample, Uma's silence on Munswamy's sarcastic comment on *hijra* makes Munswamy pause twice.

The illocutionary force in Uma's silence brings about the perlocution of silence from Munswamy.

The silence here operates as a very significant non-verbal expression of the perlocution.

Finding

The silence operates as a significant non-verbal perlocutionary act.

The radio plays display the strength in using the paralinguistic expressions and also the limitation in using the kinesic as well as the proxemic expressions.

5.9 Sample-2 (p. 40—42)

From *Collected Plays* by Mahesh Dattani (2000)

This sample brings out the concluding part of action from the play. It throws light on the mystery of Kamla's murder. Uma's investigation succeeds with Anarkali's help. However, when Uma informs it to her husband Suresh, the police superintendent, he with his senior authorities does everything needed to hush up the case. In the end Uma sums up the entire episode and the play concludes. The sample is produced below.

[sd1] **Interior. Living room of Champa.**

([sd2] *Tinkle of bells as Uma walks in.*)

ANARKALI: [u1]*Madam!*

UMA: [u2]*I am so glad you are here.* (ibid. 40)

The stage directions sd1 and sd2 give an idea of the place and Uma's entry respectively.

ANARKALI: [u3] *I am not going anywhere. I am now the head hijra. Champa has retired. She is leaving to spend the rest of her days in her sister's house in Bombay.* (ibid…)

The sense of power is sense of security too. Anarkali's comment brings out the same. Her promotion as a *'head hjjra'* creates these feelings in her mind.

UMA: [u4] *Why didn't you tell me?*

ANARKALI: [u5]*Would you have believed me? Anyway, what is the use of all that? What does it matter who killed Kamala? She is dead . . . .* [p1] *(ibid…)*

Uma's investigation is on. Anarkali's information throws light on several things in this case.

… So many times I warned her. First I thought Salim was taking her for his own pleasure. When she told me about Subbu, madam, I tried to stop her. I fought with her. I scratched her face, hoping she will become ugly and Subbu will forget her. He wanted to marry her . . . . [p2] *I was there at their wedding . . . .* [p3] *(ibid…)*

Anarkali's inputs help Uma's investigation. Kamla's relationships are seen revealed in the above citation. Also, the reactions of Anarkali to the same are revealed. Overall, Anarkali's sharing proves to be crucial in this case.

… She gave me that picture to show to Champa. I saw the men coming for her. I told her to run . . . . [p4] *([sd3] Cries for a while.) Here, madam, take this. (ibid. 41)*

The reference to the picture plays an important role in this drama. Further details of the same are seen in the following part.

UMA: [u6] *What is it?*

ANARKALI: [u7] *A special mantra is in the locket. Champa gave this to me for you. Wear it and you will be blessed with children. Sister! May you and your family be happy! Now go away, and do not come here again. Please go, sister! (*[sd4] *Silence.)* (ibid…)

Superstitions are part and parcel of the human world. This is more so in case of the characters like Anarkali, Kamla and Champa in this drama.

The following excerpt brings out some more details of the picture referred to above.

[sd5] Interior. The bedroom of Suresh and Uma.

UMA: . . . . . [p5] [u8] *The photograph was what Mr Sharma was after. A Polaroid picture that Subbu and Kamla had taken soon after their private wedding in some remote temple . . . .* [p6] *A picture of Kamla as a beautiful bride smiling at Subbu with the wedding garland around him.* (ibid…)

The photograph emerges as an evidence of Kamla's marriage with Subbu. The rest of the details of this case come out from the following part of the excerpt.

… The poojari probably didn't know that Kamla was not a woman. Of course Mr Sharma couldn't have it—[p7] *totally unacceptable. So he arranged to have Kamla burned to death. But Salim had to tell him*

about the picture. Mr Sharma simply had to have
that picture. He sent Salim to threaten Anarkali and
Champa . . . . p8 (ibid...)

Mr. Sharma uses his powers to turn the situation
in his favor. Threatening and murdering are
manifestations of the crime story in this play. In
the following part Uma informs the very vital truth
behind the crime to Suresh.

... He did get the picture eventually . . . . p9 *after losing*
his son. What a price to pay! And now he will be
arrested and tried for murder.

SURESH: u9 *I don't know . . . .* p10 (sd6 *Pause.*) *how do*
you know all this?

UMA: u10 *I have my resources.* (ibid...)

Uma succeeds in solving the case. However,
what happens next to this is quite a dramatic
development in the play.

sd7 Interior. The office of the superintendent of police.

(sd8 *Whirring of fan.*)

SURESH: u11 *Sir, that is the truth. I have my resources*
to verify all this. Of course, they are all sworn to
*secrecy so . . . .*p11 *And Mr Sharma's gratitude will be*
expressed in ways that will be, I am sure, more than
adequate p12

(sd9 *Whirring of fan stays for a while.*)
(ibid.42)

Suresh communicates the details of the case to his superior. Just ice is not only delayed, but denied too. Uma's voice over reveals the story behind the curtain. The use of voice over proves to be an important dramatic device.

UMA (sd10 *voice-over*): u12 *They knew. Anarkali, Champa and all the hijra people knew who was behind the killing of Kamla. They have no voice. The case was hushed up and was not even reported in the newspapers.* (ibid…)

The case of Kamla comes to an end quite pathetically. The remaining story is given below.

… Champa was right. The police made no arrests. Subbu's suicide was written off as an accident. The photograph was destroyed. So were the lives of two young people . . . . p13 (sd11 *Music.*) (ibid…)

The sample has following features and observations mentioned below:

5.9.1 Sample-2: features and observations

- The sample includes four different speech situations distinguished by the typical radio-play directions (see $^{sd1,\ sd5,\ sd7}$ and ^{sd10})

- Every situation has a distinct space, time and temporal setup

- The typical radio-play features like the use of 'silence' (^{sd4}), 'sounds' ($^{sd2,\ sd8}$ and ^{sd9}), 'pauses' ($_{p1\ to\ p13}$) and 'voice-over' (^{u10}), which denote and establish the following aspects of the play:

  The silence (^{sd4}): the change of the speech situation;

  The sounds (^{sd2}): the movements, i.e. proxemic action, and (^{sd8} and ^{sd10}): the place of action;

  The pauses ($_{p1}$ to $_{p13}$): the various thoughts, transmitted non-verbally;

  The voice-over (^{u10}): the thought and the action of the play, as the summary in narration.

5.9.2 Sample-2: analysis

1. Addressers and Addressees

a) Interpersonally operating

Anarkali (see $^{u1,\ u3,\ u5,\ u7;\ sd3;}$ and $_{p1\ to\ p4}$);

Uma (see $^{u2,\ u4,\ u6,\ u8,\ u10,\ u12;\ sd2,\ sd10;}$ and $_{p5,\ p6,\ p7,\ p8,\ p9,\ p13}$); and

Suresh (see $^{u9,\ u11;\ sd6;\ and}$ $_{p10,\ p11,\ p12}$).

The characters, i.e. the interpersonally operating addressers and addressees use the various utterances, pauses and actions in the stage directions to process their communication.

The frequent use of the pauses is specific to the radio performance of the play, since the radio performances are marked by the use of sounds and silences.

In all 13 pauses along with 12 utterances and 11 stage directions not only impress the statistical ratio of these communicational variants but more significantly they emerge as the salient feature of the radio plays.

Finding

The pauses mark the strength of the non-verbal communication in the radio plays.

b) Ideationally operating

i) Directly Ideational (directly from the author to the audience):

The radio directions ([sd1] to [sd11]) inform about how the author-addresser communicates his ideational address directly to the reader-addressees, the performer-addressees and the radio-addressees.

The address in the radio directions, although influenced by the features of the radio performance, displays certain features of the literary performance also.

The directions [sd1, sd5] and [sd7] inform about the various places of action (e.g. [sd1]:'Interior. Living room of Champa.'), which are normally communicated by the use of music or some other techniques specific to the radio performance.

The use of the directions ([sd1, sd5] and [sd7]) is specific more to the literary performance than a radio performance, since the author uses these directions basically to inform the places of action more directly to the readers and the actors than to the listeners of this play.

In short, the author-addresser composes his directions variedly depending upon the varied demands of the various mediums of performance.

Finding

The author-addresser's directly ideational address is influenced by certain medium-specific demands.

> **ii) Indirectly Ideational (indirectly from the author to the audience, through the characters):**

The four different speech situations in the sample communicate different indirectly ideational addresses. The author-addresser in every situation passes his message to the audience, indirectly through the characters' communication. A few of such instances are produced below:

Situation-1 (from sd1 to sd4)

The characters communicate about the mystery behind Kamla's murder.

The author indirectly communicates the success of the protagonist-investigator.

Situation-2 (from sd5 to u10)

The characters communicate about the murder investigation and in it the protagonist-investigator surprises her husband, the police-investigator.

The author indirectly communicates the failure of the police-investigator.

Situation-3 (from sd7 to sd9)

The characters communicate about hushing up Kamla's murder case.

The author indirectly communicates the injustice of the guards of justice.

Situation-4 (sd10 to sd11)

The character communicates as the mouthpiece of the author and summarizes on the unjust practices used to hush up the murder case.

The author indirectly communicates to spotlight the ghastly picture of the power politics.

Although the above discussion probes into certain shades of the author's different messages from different situations, it doesn't claim to have brought full of the messages.

2. Context

i) Socio-cultural Dimension:

The superstition in the following example operates as the socio-cultural dimension of the context.

ANARKALI: [u7] *A special mantra is in the locket. Champa gave this to me for you. Wear it and you will be blessed with children. Sister! May you and your family be happy!*

The superstition of the bliss of mantra in the locket is a socio-cultural reality that functions as the context, in which Anarkali's communication gets certain meaning.

As this particular contextual dimension plays a decisive role to make the utterance meaningful, all the addressers' and addressees' shared knowledge of the same can facilitate the meaning making process.

ii) Literary Dimension:

The use of [sd1,] [sd5] and [sd7] displays a literary technique into operation as the literary dimension of the context. The above-referred directions, as a literary convention, inform about the different places of action in the different speech situations. The use of this literary technique offers the context in which the speech in these situations becomes meaningful.

The following example throws light on this operation.

[sd7] **Interior. The office of the superintendent of police.**

SURESH: [u11] *Sir, that is the truth. I have my resources to verify all this. Of course, they are all sworn to secrecy so . . . .* [p11] *And Mr Sharma's gratitude will be expressed in ways that will be, I am sure, more than adequate . . .* [p12]

On the basis of the information shared with the audience in [sd7] the utterance [u11] becomes meaningful. Without knowing this information, it can be difficult to draw inferences on [u11]. Hence, the literary technique of using [sd7] operates as the context, in which the utterance [u11] becomes meaningful.

iii) Theatrical Dimension:

The radio-specific technique of the voice over used in [sd10] functions as the theatrical dimension of the context. In the literary performance the information: '*UMA* ([sd10] *voice-over*):', and in the radio performance its phonetic execution play the contextual role, which helps the addressees' interpretation of the utterance [u12].

Without sharing this context, it can be difficult for the addressees to process the interpretation of the utterance [u12] in isolation.

The use of sounds like the tinkle of bells ([sd2]) and the whirring of fan ([sd8] and [sd9]) establish the places of actions respectively, Champa's room and the office of the police superintendent. The further part of the action takes place in the context of these places of action.

The use of these sounds here operates as the 'contextual cues' (Kramsch: 1998: 27)

3. Speech acts

i) <u>Locutionary act</u>

a) **Phonetic act:** The phonetic act is discussed here with the help of the following examples. The phonetic execution of the utterances *'Madam!'* in [u1] and *'Sir'* in [u11] is obviously influenced by politeness, whereas the utterance [u12], being a voice over, is influenced by the specific convention of its phonetic execution in the radio performance.

So, the phonetic acts of executing [u1] and [u11] are influenced by the politeness principle and that of the [u12] is influenced by the performance-specific convention of the voice-over.

<u>Finding</u>

The variations in the execution of the phonetic acts are the results of the factors like the pragmatic principles and the theatrical conventions influencing the execution process.

b) **Phatic act:** As the phatic act of saying something is represented grammatically, the dashes indicating the pauses [p1] to [p13] strengthen the various locutionary functions of expressing something, what is not effectively expressed verbally alone.

For instance, in the following utterance, a particular use of the grammatical structure, with the pause $_{p10}$ between the two sentences, facilitates the performance of the phatic act.

SURESH: [u9] *I don't know . . . . $_{p10}$ (Pause.) how do you know all this?*

The most vital aspect to be communicated by the above utterance is how Suresh is surprised not to know something, what Uma knows, and it is significant that the surprise is not effectively communicated verbally, as much it is communicated in combination with the use of the pause $_{p10.}$

Grammatically, the pause $_{p10}$ in the utterance [u9] connects a statement with a question, both of which independently do not communicate the surprise on the part of Suresh. The 'surprise' is expressed effectively, only with the use of the pause between the two sentences.

Like the two sentences, even the pause $_{p10}$ does not express the 'surprise' independently, but in combination with the two sentences only.

The composition of these two sentences, with the pause between them, has a certain grammatical structure, which helps the performance of the present phatic act of expressing the 'surprise'.

In this sense, the grammar proves to be 'complementary' (Leech: 1983: X) to the pragmatic operation of the locutionary (phatic) act, by facilitating the expression of the illocutionary force of the 'surprise' hereby.

Finding

Certain 'complementary' grammatical structures facilitate the performance of the speech acts.

c) Rhetic act:

The act of performing [u12] is the performance of a rhetic act, as it employs the literary and the rhetorical device of effective narration. With the effective narrative technique used in [u12], the addresser summarizes the total action to conclude the play.

The perception of the message that the utterance [u12] communicates is semantically derivable and rhetorically facilitated.

As the semantically derivable message is facilitated rhetorically, the process of the perception operates pragmatically, since the rhetoric facilitation here performs an illocutionary function 'in' (Austin: 1962: 120) communicating the message.

Finding

The rhetic act pragmatically operates the perception process of the message, which is derivable semantically and facilitated rhetorically.

ii) **Illocutionary act**

   a) **Verbal Forces:** e.g. The force of the success transmitted verbally in the utterance [u10] is discussed here.

UMA: [u10] *I have my resources.*

The transmission of the above utterance is the transmission of the force of Uma's success in unveiling the brutal act of the social system (including her own family members) that tries to hush up the murder case of Kamla.

It is against the utter brutality of the act that the force of success strongly evolves from the utterance.

So, the intensity of the force of success is born out of the intensity of the force of brutality.

Precisely, the force is communicated against its anti-force. The greater the anti-force, the better the communication of the present verbal force. In this sense, both these forces are directly proportional to each other and operate in the opposite directions showing a centrifugal trend i.e. moving away from the center between them.

Finding

Certain pragmatic forces and their anti-forces are directly proportional to each other in their operation.

These forces operate in the opposite directions showing a centrifugal trend.

b) **Non-verbal Forces** (kinesic, paralinguistic, and proxemic): The non-verbal illocutionary forces are discussed here with the functioning of the pauses in the sample, e.g. the pauses $_{p1, p2, p4}$ and $_{p13}$.

There is a non-verbal force of helplessness that emerges neither kinesically, nor paralinguistically, nor proxemically, but out of the pauses $_{p1, p2, p4}$ and $_{p13}$, as seen below.

1. *'What does it matter who killed Kamala? She is dead . . . . $_{p1}$'*
2. *'He wanted to marry her . . . . $_{p2}$'*
3. *'I told her to run . . . . $_{p4}$'*
4. *'The photograph was destroyed. So were the lives of two young people . . . . $_{p13}$'*

All the four pauses above express the force of helplessness coming out of the situations, where the characters have no choices and they are seen at a point of no return. Considering the 'felicity conditions' (Grundi: 2000: 273), it is found that the force becomes meaningful in the context of the utterance and the felicity conditions, and not by the expression of the pauses, in isolation.

Precisely, the non-verbal forces operate in the context of the utterances and the felicity conditions processing their communication.

Finding

The non-verbal force of pauses functions not in isolation but in the context of the utterances and the felicity conditions processing their communication.

iii) Perlocutionary act

a) **Verbal Expressions:** e.g. The utterance [u5] operates as the verbal expression of the perlocution delivered in response to [u4].

UMA: [u4] Why didn't you tell me?

ANARKALI: [u5]*Would you have believed me? Anyway, what is the use of all that? What does it matter who killed Kamala?*

The perlocution in [u5] operates as the response to the indirect speech act used in [u4] by Uma, who asks Anarkali to tell her something she wants to know. Initially the doubts in [u4] are responded to by the doubts in [u5], however later, the expected explanation follows.

The perlocutionary act in [u5] again shows here the expected and the unexpected responses operating in it.

Finding

The perlocutionary acts can have both the expected and the unexpected responses.

b) **Non-verbal Expressions** (kinesic, paralinguistic, and proxemic): The sample shows a few non-verbal expressions functioning as the perlocutionary acts. For instance, Anarkali's *'crying'* in [sd3] is a paralinguistically operating non-verbal perlocution to the utterance [u4].

UMA: [u4] *Why didn't you tell me?*

ANARKALI: [u5]*Would you have believed me? Anyway, what is the use of all that? . . . .* ([sd3] *Cries for a while.*)

Except for this example ([sd3]), the sample doesn't show any other paralinguistic, kinesic or proxemic operations of perlocutionary acts. However, some other examples of the non-verbal perlocutions are found in the form of the pauses, e.g. the pauses [p1, p2, p3] and [p4] operate as the non-verbal perlocutionary acts in response to the utterance [u4].

With the speech situation analyzed above, the analysis of the speech situations from *Seven Steps Around The Fire* completes. The total work of the analysis in the thesis also completes here.

5.10 Conclusion

This chapter works out the analysis of the speech situations from two plays, *Ghashiram Kotwal* (Tendulkar: 2000) and *Seven Steps Around The Fire* (Dattani: 2000). The diversity in the forms of these two plays is found reflected in the operational mechanism of the speech situations as well. The form of the radio play evolves certain form-specific findings. The major findings from this chapter as well as from the previous chapter of Analysis are generalized and discussed in the next chapter of Conclusions.

CHAPTER-6
CONCLUSIONS

6.1 Preliminaries

$\textbf{T}$he present chapter generalizes the findings evolved from the analysis of the speech situations. The generalized findings are classified under two types of conclusions, the general conclusions and the component-specific conclusions. Besides the conclusions, the chapter also includes pedagogical implications and future possibilities of research. General conclusions are as follows:

6.2 General conclusions

1. Either of the components, viz. the space, the time, the topic and the temporal setup, or all of them together operate/s as the marker/s to distinguish—though not to define and demark—one speech situation from another in drama.

2. The operational modes of all the components of a speech situation are found holistically centralized in the message transmission. Hence to assess 'message'

is to assess all the other components centralized in it. Thus 'message' evolves as the central component.

3. The radio plays, and also the other types of plays, have certain medium-specific strengths and limitations, which influence the author-addresser's communication, and thereby determine both the composition and the transmission of the speech situations.

4. The stage directions in drama bring out the context of the interpersonal communication between the author-addresser and the reader-addressees, and the performer-addressees; and also bring out the context of the ideational communication between the author-addresser and the viewer-addressees, the tele-viewer addressees, and the audio-addressees.

5. In drama, there can be any pivotal speech situation that offers context to many other speech situations in the play, and to the whole action of the play.

6. The speech situations in the print form of drama—as compared to the theatrical and the other forms of drama—are more cognitive than sensory in the perceptual channel of the reader-addressees' experience of it.

6.3 Component-specific conclusions

The component-specific conclusions are discussed below with the same sequence used for the analysis of the components: the addressers and addressees, the context, the speech acts, and their subcomponents.

6.3.1 Addressers and addressees

On the basis of the analysis, it is observed that the component addressers and addressees is influenced by the technique of multiple characters played by the same interlocutor, the gimmicks and conventions, the terms of address, the interlocutors' juxtaposition of the various contexts and the various worlds, and the medium-specific operational dynamics of the speech situations in drama.

The dramatic technique of 'the same performer playing the multiple roles' brings out certain variations. In *Ghashiram Kotwal,* it appears as a typical feature of Indian theatre, where the '*Sutradhar*' plays the multiple roles (see sample-2, *Ghashiram Kotwal*). In *Evam Indrajit*, the same technique operates as a means to highlight the theme of identity crisis and the instrumental status (see sample-2, *Evam Indrajit*) of the 'dramatis personae' (see Abrams, 1957: 124). *The Dread Departure* and *Naga-Mandala* also display the instrumental status of the characters operating through the same technique of the multiple characters played by the same performer.

The performers playing such instrumental roles 'in saying' (Austin, 1962: 120) or communicating the author's message, perform an illocutionary function in the author's communication to his audiences.

However, *Naga-Mandala* also displays the originality of the performers as addressers and addressees. *'Appanna's house'* in this play is established not so much as per the author's instructions, as much by the originality of the performer's roles.

In case of establishing the details of the house—especially regarding its interior and the exterior—not mentioned in the script and yet established in the performance, the performing-addressers, especially the director and the back-stage-artists, add something of their own to the message. Thus, **these performing-addressers do not remain merely instrumental** in conveying the author's address, **but get the originality as the addressers** in communicating details of the house.

As they communicate through the established house, their communication functions as a message-transmission through the 'artifacts' i.e. DISCOURSE by means of ARTIFACTS by means of NO TEXT but by means of the PERFORMING-ADDRESSERS' ROLE.

As the above-referred performing-addressers operate so, more or less, the other performing-addressers like the music-man, the light-man, the make-up-man and the costume designer also operate in the same way. Initially they are the addressees of the author-addresser, however they undergo a remarkable transition from the addressees to the addressers, while performing their roles. Thus, **the performer-addressees turn out to be the performing-addressers.**

The use of the **theatrical gimmicks** e.g. the presence of Bhaurao's soul suggested through the *'Bier at the centre-stage'* in *The Dread Departure*; and the use of certain conventions like the 'dramatic irony' (Abrams: 1957: 82) and the 'aside' (Abrams: 1957: 159) throw light on some new dimensions of the component, addressers and addressees. The very role of Bhaurao's soul, as an addresser and addressee operating through the gimmicks and the above dramatic conventions, evolves a new dimension as **a supposed virtual addresser and addressee, who operates physically.**

In some speech situations it is observed that some characters, though absent in a given speech situation, influence its operational mechanism. For instance, Appanna is neither an addresser nor an addressee in some speech situations in *Naga-Mandala*, and yet remarkably influences the speech in particular and the situations in general.

The role of the performing addressers (the actors) is observed to be interpersonal in their communication with each other; and both interpersonal and ideational in their communication with the audiences. The utterances issued by Rani and Kurudavva in *Naga-Mandala* prove their roles, as the addressers and addressees operating interpersonally with each other, and also as the addressers operating both interpersonally and ideationally especially with the viewer-addressees.

The use of the terms of address influences certain operational aspects of the speech situations. In Mahesh Dattani's *Seven Steps around the Fire*, the different pronouns (*'she'* and *'it'*) used by the different addressers (Uma and Munswamy respectively) for the same addressee (Anarkali, the eunuch) facilitate all the addressees' (the character addressed in the play as well as the readers, viewers and all the addressees) perception of the addressers' different points of view and their different attitudes (Uma's respectful attitude and Munswamy's malicious one) in the same situation towards the same addressee, *hijra*, the eunuch.

Hence, the inferences regarding the attitudes of the addressers and addressees are influenced by the use of the terms of address.

It is also observed that **the addressers and addressees emerge as the connecting factors between the literary, the theatrical and the societal worlds.** In Badal Sircar's *Evam Indrajit* (sample-1), the addressers and addressees ('Auntie', 'Writer', 'Manasi' and the 'Four Men') operate at the different contextual levels of the different worlds in the same speech situation. Similarly in Alekar's *The Dread Departure* the author-addresser directly influences the theatrical performance by instructing about the sound effects, the actions and the space distancing of the actors (the performing addressers). Thus, by directly influencing the theatrical performance, **the author-addresser juxtaposes the literary and the theatrical performances, and thereby, also key controls these performances.**

The radio plays influence the addressers and addressees with certain medium-specific strengths and limitations of their own. For instance, the author-addresser's ideational address is influenced by certain medium-specific techniques. The radio directions in *Seven Steps around the Fire* inform about the various places of action, which are normally established at the radio-addressees' cognitive level by the use of music or some other techniques, specific to the radio performance, e.g. the *'Interior. Living room of Champa.'* is established and communicated by the *'Tinkle of bells'*. Thus, **the medium-specific strengths and limitations of drama influence the author-addresser's ideational communication, and thereby determine both the composition and the transmission of the speech situations.**

Besides the use of music, **the pauses also mark the strength of the non-verbal address in the radio plays.**

6.3.2 The context

The conclusions associated with the context are generalized under three types.

1. Socio-cultural dimension of the context
2. Literary dimension of the context
3. Theatrical dimension of the context

6.3.2.1 Socio-cultural dimension of the context

Karnad's *Naga-Mandala* evolves Indian folklore, as the socio-cultural dimension of the context in the play. **The Indian folklore operates as a connecting factor between the real world, literary and theatrical worlds.** Whereas, in Alekar's *The Dread Departure*, the socio-cultural practices like 'the rituals after death' operate as the shared knowledge i.e. the context in the addressees' perception of the speech situation.

Tendulkar's *Ghashiram Kotwal* proves: **if a situation has some fuzzy logic operating at the contextual level, the action processed in it results into an absurd manifestation of the same.** The socio-cultural custom of celebrating 'the victory of the good over the evil' is taken illogically here by the crowd, who celebrate Ghashiram's death.

The Crowd's mistaken or the fuzzy logic, based only on their partial knowledge of the reality, establishes Nana as the icon of 'the good', and Ghashiram as the icon of 'the evil'. The icons are an outcome of the Crowd's illogical thinking. Hence, the celebration on Ghashiram's death is absurd.

In Badal Sircar's *Evam Indrajit* the social class and its mentality ('the bureaucratic mentality of the middle class'), the place of the action ('*office*') and the setting (Kolkatta), compose the socio-cultural context of the speech situations. Apart from this, the socio-cultural dimension of the motherly affection for a son (between Auntie and the Writer) functions as the context in the same play. However, the relationship between the Writer and Auntie is not only a typical Indian socio-cultural reality, but the same is found in the various cultures all over the world. In this sense, **the present point of the socio-cultural context gets certain universal application.**

6.3.2.2 Literary dimension of the context

The literary dimension of the context is manifested through the shared knowledge of the various literary devices and the techniques in drama. The catchy and effective use of 'Manasi', as the Writer's inspiration personified in Badal Sircar's *Evam Indrajit*, and especially the 'fantastic element' projected through it, elevate the same to the status of the gimmicks used in drama. **The shared**

knowledge of the literary gimmick operates the contextual dimension here.

In the same play, the broken communication manifests the absurdities in the modern life. The audiences' shared knowledge of this literary feature attains the status of the context, which obviously facilitates their perception of the speech situation.

Similarly, the literary and the theatrical conventions of the use of the chorus in *Ghashiram Kotwal* also operate as the context. The conclusion of the play is anticipated due to the conventional action of merging all the characters into the chorus. The very formation of the chorus, which is a contextual aspect here, communicates the conclusion earlier than the concerned utterance does the same.

In this process of communication, **the role of the context is found to be not only complementary to the use of the utterance, but comparable with the same as well.**

6.3.2.3 Theatrical dimension of the context

The various theatrical conventions, being part of the shared knowledge between the various addressers and addressees, emerge as the context and operate as the 'contextualization cues' (Kramsch, 1998: 27) for the addressees, in speech situations. In Alekar's *The Dread Departure*, the speech situations are processed in the context created by the use of the light effects, the stage property and some other theatrical devices. For instance, the spotlight on the '*two Men in quarrel*' highlights their communication and the area unnecessary for the same is faded out by darkening the rest of the stage.

The gimmicks used in the theatre emerge as the context in the process of the communication in drama. Badal Sircar's *Evam Indrajit* uses a theatrical gimmick of calling the spectators from the auditorium, and thus invites their participation in the performance. The speech situation is processed in the context of this gimmick.

The use of the artifacts in the same play, e.g. the stool and the duster used by the Peon; and the chair, the table and the telephone used by the Boss, create the ambience required to establish the two different identities of the same performer, as the Peon and as the Boss in the office. Thus, **the use of the situation-specific stage property develops the situation-specific ambience, to establish the speech situation theatrically.**

6.3.3 Speech acts

The conclusions are presented here under various types and subtypes of the speech acts mentioned below:

6.3.3.1 Locutionary speech act

a. Phonetic speech act
b. Phatic speech act
c. Rhetic speech act

6.3.3.2 Illocutionary speech act

a. Verbal forces
b. Non-verbal forces

6.3.3.3 Perlocutionary speech act

a. Verbal expressions
b. Non-verbal expressions

6.3.3.1 Locutionary speech act

a. Phonetic speech act

The conclusions with regard to the phonetic speech acts are drawn here from the literary performances. Hence, obviously, the assessment of the phonetic execution has its own limitations. However, it is observed that certain literary, grammatical and medium-specific devices influence the process of the phonetic execution of the utterances in drama. Hence, on the basis of such devices, the conclusions could be drawn as follows:.

For instance, in Karnad's *Naga-Mandala*, **the phonetic acts are brought out by the use of the grammatical devices** (the phatic acts): the interjection followed by an exclamatory mark (*'Ah!'*); and the Wh-question (*'What happened?'*) and the imperative sentence (*'Tell us!'*). The primary stress on the interjection *'Ah!'* expressing the weariness of New Flame is a phonetic act noticed through the use of the exclamatory mark following the interjection. The two examples of an obviously falling tone executed at the end of the Wh-question, *'What happened?',* and at the end of the imperative sentence, *'Tell us!'*, are also the phonetic acts assessed on the basis of the grammatical devices.

The radio play *Seven Steps around the Fire* evolves two very distinctive operations of the same phonetic speech act, depending upon the two different mediums of performance: literary and radio.

A stage direction in this play: *'A scream. The flames engulf the scream.'* is an act 'of saying' a lot metaphorically, without saying it phonetically in the literary medium. Whereas, in the radio transmission, the phonetic execution of the *'screaming'* is supposed to operate initially at a high pitch, and later, muffled by the sound of the flames. The execution of the same phonetic act in the radio transmission is an execution of a paralinguistic sound of screaming jointly composed with the musical sound of the flames.

Precisely, the metaphorical 'act of saying' in the literary performance, emerges as the counterpart of the joint paralinguistic and musical 'acts of saying' in the radio performance.

Hence, **the locutionary phonetic act 'of saying' the same shows certain medium—specific distinct modes of execution.**

In the same play, the phonetic acts 'of saying' (*'Madam!'* and *'Sir!'*) are obviously influenced by the politeness principle; whereas, the *'voice over'* executed with the loud and the echoed volume in the play shows the influence of the medium-specific conventions of the radio transmission.

Badal Sircar's *Evam Indrajit* shows that the phonetic act is influenced by the use of the pauses; and **the pauses** (the *'no responses'* from the Writer) **and the rising intonation** (Auntie's expression of irritation due to the Writer's *'no responses'*) **are found in an alternate sequence in the execution of their phonetic speech acts.**

In the same play, the monotonous calls, repeatedly given to Harish by Amal, Kamal, Vimal and Indrajit, arouse certain phonetic monotony. **The phonetic monotony is judged here on the basis of the compositional monotony; and the act of using the compositional monotony is the author's act that directs the characters' act of executing the phonetic monotony.**

b. Phatic speech act

The phatic acts in drama are mainly found in a complementary role to the other acts of the verbal and the non-verbal communication. In Badal Sircar's *Evam Indrajit*, the phatic act is found in the repeatedly used structures of questioning, which create an illocutionary force of nothingness e.g. the Writer's worry, *'nothing to write about'* , questioned by Manasi, and the counter questioning by the Writer (*'What shall I write? Who shall I write about? How many people do I know? And what do I know about them?'*). The phatic act here proves to be complementary to the function of the illocutionary act. Also in Dattani's *Seven Steps around the Fire* certain grammatical structures play the complementary role to the performance of the speech acts (e.g. *SURESH: I don't know . . . . (Pause.) how do you know all this?*). Structurally, the pause connects the statement with the question, and functionally, it brings out *Suresh's* surprise. The 'surprise' is expressed effectively with the structural composition of the two sentences with the pause between them, which helps the performance of communicating the 'force of surprise'. In this sense, **grammar proves to be—what Leech calls—'complementary' (Leech: 1983: X) to the pragmatic operation of the locutionary (phatic) act by facilitating the expression of the illocutionary force of the 'surprise'.**

As far as the print form of drama is concerned, it is observed that **in the process of reader-addressee's perception, the grammatical devices operate as a linking factor between the locution and the illocution of the concerned utterances.** In Karnad's *Naga-Mandala* (sample-1) a punctuation (exclamatory) mark following the interjection '*Ah*' (the locution) determines the weariness (the illocution) of New Flame in [u3]; and the sentence types (the Wh-question and the imperative sentence) in [u4], and (the two Wh-questions) in [u6], determine the excitement (the illocution) of all Flames to know the further part of New Flame's narration of the 'Story'.

Similarly, in *Evam Indrajit*, the use of the structural monotony reflects the real-life monotony. And the author-addresser's act of using the structural monotony links up the reader-addressees' perception to the performing-addressers' act of expressing the real-life monotony.

The findings discussed above, strikingly evolve **the non-verbal form and the function of the phatic act,** as a feature of the print form of drama. *Seven Steps around the Fire* underlines it in the form and the function of the pause in Munswamy's utterance: '*Madam, if you don't mind me saying, why is a lady from a respectable family like yourself . . . .* $_{p2}$?' The locution in the phatic act of pausing can be inferred (on the basis of Munswamy's attitudes manifested in the play towards the *hijra* community) as, 'Madam*, if you don't mind me saying, why is a lady from a respectable family like yourself should <u>at all involve in the cases of the hijras?</u>'

The underlined part is a supposed verbal counterpart of the act of pausing, inferred so. Hence, **the phatic 'act of saying' something metaphorically and non-verbally is traceable here from the 'act of saying' nothing phonetically and verbally.**

The discussion on the phatic act sums up with a generalization that since the grammatical devices are non-verbal in their form and function, **the phatic locution is a non-verbal locution**—i.e. the non-verbal aspect of the locutionary speech act—which is complementary to various verbal and the non-verbal acts of communication, holistically operating in the print form of drama.

c. Rhetic speech act

In the process of the communication in drama, the rhetic speech acts are also found in a holistic mode of operation with the other speech acts, what evolves the rhetic acts to be complementary to the other speech acts. All the analyzed plays in general and *Evam Indrajit* in particular prove it. For instance:

AUNTIE: [u5] *Do what you want. Night and day—scribble, scribble, scribble. No food, no drink, just scribble. Only God knows what will come out of all this scribbling . . . .* [p4]

The rhetic act operates here through the rhetorical device of repetition. The repetition of the utterance *'scribble'* transmits an illocutionary force of apathy against the very act of *'scribbling'*. Hence, **the rhetic act of repetition proves to be complementary to the illocutionary function of the act.**

In the same play, the act of repetition brings in rhythm, which is another rhetorical device, e.g.

'WRITER: (^{sd2} *Coming downstage.)* ^{u1} *From home to school. From school to college. From college to the world. The world is an office. Like this one. A lot of business is transacted here—very important business. A lot of people work here—Amal, Vimal, Kamal and Indrajit.'*

The utterance opens with three identical structures and also ends with two sentences identically structured that make the narration rhythmic and effective. Here, the phatic act (the structures) and the rhetic act (the rhythmic narration) are found in a holistic operation. And using such techniques is the author's act that helps the character's act of the effective narration. Here, the characters' acts are interpersonal, whereas, the author's acts are ideational. In this sense, **the characters' interpersonal speech acts come out of the author's ideational 'non-speech acts'** (Leech, 1983: 214) in the process of communication.

The repetition emerges as the major device to perform the locutionary (rhetic) speech acts; and the playwright's rhetic non-speech acts evolve the characters' locutionary and illocutionary speech acts, which eventually bring about the perlocutions on the part of all the addressees.

As a result, the author-addresser emerges as the chief addresser, whereas the interpersonal interlocutors (e.g. the *Writer* in *Evam Indrajit* and the *Flames and Man* in Karnad's *Naga-Mandala*) remain instrumental in the ideational process of the message communication in drama.

6.3.3.2 Illocutionary speech act

a. Verbal force

The verbal illocutionary forces in drama are found influenced by certain factors like the relationship of the addressers and the addressees, the complementary operation of the various speech acts, the forces, the anti-forces and their trends in the operation, the cultural context, the rhetorical devices like repetition, the type of the dramatic performance, and the pragmatic operations like implicatures, turn taking etc.

In *Evam Indrajit* the commands by the office bearers to the Peon manifest how the relationship of the interlocutors influences the verbal forces, e.g. '*Bring me a glass of water.*'; '*Bring me a betel-leaf and zarda.*'; '*Two cigarettes—'Scissors'!*' etc. The force of the commands emerges out of the awareness about the hierarchical difference between the master and the servant relationship. **The verbal force proves to be the product of the interlocutors' relationship** here.

In the same play, the verbal force of absurdity is manifested in the complementary operation of the phatic act and the rhetic act. The phatic act of a particular pattern of questioning brings out the force of nothingness (the Writer has no topic for 'writing'); and the rhetic act of using the device of repetition brings out the force of (Auntie's) apathy towards the 'writing'. The two forces complement each other to collectively bring out the verbal force of absurdity in the play.

The play *Seven Steps around the Fire* proves that **certain pragmatic forces have their anti-forces and they are directly proportional to each other in their operation.** The play also shows that **these forces operate in the opposite directions showing a centrifugal trend.**

For instance, the force of success transmitted verbally in the following utterance, *UMA:* [u10] *I have my resources* (to investigate the murder case of *Kamla*). Uma unveils the brutal act of Kamla's murder. The force of Uma's success in investigation and the force of the brutality in murdering stand against each other as the force and its anti-force respectively. So, the intensity of the force of the success is born out of the intensity of the anti-force of the brutality. Hence, the greater is the anti-force, the better the communication of the present verbal force. In this sense, both these forces are directly proportional to each other and operate in the opposite directions, showing a centrifugal trend, i.e. moving away from the center between them.

The verbal illocutionary force in using the utterance *'hijra'* in the same play proves that the intensity of the strong pejorative force, in using the utterance *'hijra'* in Indian languages, is perceivable only in its Indian socio-cultural context. It is observed here that **the intensity of the verbal force is language specific, and the interpretation of language is culture-specific, hence the intensity of the verbal force is culture-specific.**

The perception of the intensity of the verbal force is influenced also by the devices like repetition. In *Ghashiram Kotwal* it is observed that **the verbal 'sense' gets transformed into the verbal 'force', when certain verbal expressions are used repeatedly and perceived collectively,** e.g. the verbal force of wrath of Ghashiram, exerted against the Crowd, and also against himself. In expressing his anger, Ghashiram repeatedly uses the utterances like *'hit,* *beat*, *spit*, *crush*, *crack*, *cut off*, *cowards*, *scared*, *dare*, *come on'* etc. Each of these utterances communicates the 'sense' of the anger independently, whereas they communicate the 'force' of the anger, when used repeatedly and perceived collectively.

The type of the dramatic performance influences the operational mode of the verbal force. *Ghashiram Kotwal* proves that the verbal force that has a literary mode of operation in the print form operates with a phonetic mode in a theatrical performance. Thus, the verbal force has a performance-specific operational mode. The force of the opening prayer (*'nandi'*) in the play comes out through the rhyme (e.g. the rhyme scheme of [u1]: a-a, b-c, d-c, e-e, f-f, g-h), the rhythm, and the repetition ([sd3]), which are basically the literary devices, used as the acts in delivering the force of the prayer. In a theatrical performance, the verbal force in these literary devices comes out phonetically through the varied intonation patterns. And so, the radio performance and the tele-visual performance and such other performance types can also have their own operational mode in the delivery of the verbal force.

Karnad's *Naga-Mandala* proves the influence of certain pragmatic operations like 'implicature' (Grundi, 2000: 273) and 'turn taking' (Grundi: 2000: 276) on the execution of the verbal forces. For instance,

FLAME 1: [u2] *You are late. It is well past midnight.*

NEW FLAME: [u3] *Ah! There was such a to-do in our house tonight.*

The force of Flame-1's enquiry regarding New Flame's late coming is the implicature of enquiry, operating as questioning through statements, and confirmed in the turn taking of New Flame, as cited above.

The implicature facilitates the transmission of the force, whereas the turn taking facilitates the perception of the force.

b. Non-verbal force

The non-verbal illocutionary forces in the print form of drama are influenced by the various dimensions of the context, the verbal forces, the devices like repetition, certain pragmatic operations like the 'felicity conditions' (Grundi, 2000: 273), and the type of performance etc.

Naga-Mandala proves that **the context of the non-verbal forces determines their mode of manifestation.** It is observed that certain kinesic, proxemic and paralinguistic manifestations of certain non-verbal forces are obviously assumable on the basis of their context, e.g. the stage direction, '*A new Flame enters and is enthusiastically greeted.*' The playwright does not mention any particular verbal or the non-verbal mode of welcoming here, and yet, some kinesic, proxemic, paralinguistic or the mode combining all these together, is certainly assumable in this act of welcoming. The mode is assumable here on the basis of the socio-cultural context of such customs in the society.

The non-verbal forces and the verbal forces are found in a complementary operation in *Ghashiram Kotwal.* The non-verbal force operating proxemically in the act of 'dancing' in the play (e.g. in the '*nandi*') proves to be complementary to the verbal force of the utterance 'prancing', since the steps of the 'dancing' are the proxemic manifestation of the force of the 'prancing'.

The same play also proves that **the non-verbal 'sense' gets transformed into the non-verbal 'force', when certain non-verbal actions are used repeatedly and perceived collectively.** The non-verbal force of the Crowd's ecstatic cheer in the play comes out kinesically, paralinguistically and proxemically due to the repeatedly transmitted and the collectively perceived actions: '*The mob yells* ([sd4]), *The mob shouts*

(^{sd5}), *The crowd's shouting continues* (^{sd5}), *The crowd cheers* (^{sd6}), *The crowd shouts. Cheers* (^{sd8}), *The crowd dances* (^{sd8})' etc.

Each of these non-verbal actions communicates the 'sense' of the cheer independently. They communicate the ecstatic 'force' of the cheer, when used repeatedly and perceived collectively.

In *Seven Steps around the Fire*, it is proved that **the felicity conditions and the context process the non-verbal force of the pauses in drama.**

The non-verbal force of helplessness in the following utterances emerges neither kinesically, nor paralinguistically, nor proximically but out of the pauses $_{p1, \ p2, \ p3}$ and $_{p4}$.

1. *'What does it matter who killed Kamala? She is dead . . . . $_{p1}$'*
2. *'He wanted to marry her . . . . $_{p2}$'*
3. *'I told her to run . . . . $_{p3}$'*
4. *'The photograph was destroyed. So were the lives of two young people . . . . $_{p4}$'*

All the four pauses express the force of helplessness, coming out of the situations, where the characters have no choices and they are seen at a point of no return. Considering these felicity conditions, it is found that the force becomes meaningful in the context of the utterance and the felicity conditions.

Evam Indrajit shows that **the transmission mode of the non-verbal forces varies as the type of the performance varies.** The stage direction, *'Changing files from the 'In' tray to the 'Out' and back again.'* communicates a kinesically transmitted force of the mechanical routine of the middle-class bureaucrats, as the same action is repeated frequently. The device of repetition operates kinesically in the theatrical performance, whereas, the same operates rhetorically in the literary performance. In this sense, **the kinesic transmission of the force in a theatrical performance operates as a counterpart to the rhetorical transmission of the same in the literary performance.**

6.3.3.3 Perlocutionary speech act

a. Verbal expressions

The verbal expressions of the perlocutionary acts are marked by the influence of certain pragmatic principles, the multiplicity in manifesting the same act, the instrumental role of the interlocutors, the multiple speech acts etc.

The Dread Departure shows that both **the illocutions and the perlocutions violate the 'cooperative principle'** (Leech: 1983:

16) and **the 'politeness principle'** (Leech, 1983: 16). It is proved in the following utterances.

'*MAN 2:* [u2] *You watch your mouth.*

MAN 1: [u3] *Shut up! Don't think to scare me!*'

In the context of the quarrel, Man-1 showing uncooperativeness, impoliteness, anger, and warning in [u3], can be called a perlocution to the force of warning and anger delivered by Man-2 in [u2].

The play also shows that **the perlocutions (**in the [u3] above**) again operate as the locutions and the illocutions to cause new perlocutions and the same recurs cyclically throughout the speech situation**. The perlocution in [u3] operates as a locutionary act, which executes the illocutionary force of warning and anger causing the perlocution (of a strong disagreement in [u4])as follows:

'*MAN 2:* [u4] *I am all grown up! I don't need you to show me anything!*'

It is observed here that **the speech acts recur in a cyclic trend**.

Ghashiram Kotwal evolves a very intricate trend of multiplicity in the manifestation of the perlocutionary speech acts. Sutradhar's utterance, '[u7] *Who are you?*' generates twelve different verbal responses in the '*nandi*' of this play. Thus, even single utterance can arouse multiple verbal responses in such a speech situation. However, the function of the perlocutionary act performed by each is the same i.e. the act of self introduction. This shows that the multiple verbal responses can perform the same and single perlocutionary act. These two findings together evolve a new finding: **the same and single utterance can arouse the same and single perlocutionary act manifested through the multiple verbal expressions.**

An opposite kind of trend to this is found in *Evam Indrajit*. On the one hand, *Ghashiram Kotwal* shows the trend of the single utterance generating multiple verbal responses, whereas, on the other hand, *Evam Indrajit* shows **the opposite trend of the multiple utterances generating single verbal response**.

For instance,

AMAL: [u12] *Hareesh . . .*

VIMAL: [u13] *Hareesh . . .*

KAMAL: [u14] *Hareesh . . .*

INDRAJIT: [u15] *Hareesh . . .*

AMAL: ([sd9] *A little more loudly.*) [u16] *Hareesh . . .*

WRITER: [u17] *Yes, Sir.*

It is proved here that **the same (and single verbal) response** ([u17]) **operates as a collective perlocution to the same (and single) utterance transmitted** ([u12, u13, u14, u15] and [u16]) **by the multiple addressers.**

Ghashiram Kotwal brings out some more significant findings like **the characters' varied perlocutionary acts 'of their own' are in fact not of their own but are the pre-planned part of the overall decorum of the play.** Thus, the operation of the speech situation in general, and the characters' perlocutionary acts in particular, are influenced by the factor of performing or showcasing for the audience, as per the scheme of the play; and the act of performing for the audience emerges as an instrumental act of the performance. All these findings are typical features of the speech situations in drama.

For instance, '*The End*' in Sutradhar's utterance [u1]: '*And in the end came The End.*' clearly hints at 'performing for audience' the end of Ghashiram's life and powers, as well as the end of the play.

As a response to the same hint, all the characters perform '*The End*' by performing the various perlocutionary acts, which are different from each other's.

The verbally transmitted perlocutionary acts are [u3, u4, u5,] by Ghashiram, [u6, u7] by Nana and [u8] by All together. By performing [u3, u4, u5,] Ghashiram meets '*The End*' of his reign and life; by performing [u6] and [u7], Nana brings about '*The End*' of Ghashiram's powers; whereas, by performing [u8], All together showcase '*The End*' of the play.

b. **The non-verbal expressions**

The non-verbal expressions studied in the thesis show the features like the multiple functions of the same speech act, the holistic operation of the verbal and the non-verbal perlocutionary acts, the influence of the author's non-speech act on the characters' non-verbal perlocutionary act, and the strength of silence as a non-verbal perlocutionary expression in the radio plays.

The play *Naga-Mandala* evolves the multiple functions of the same non-verbal expressions. For instance,

'MAN: ([sd1]*To the audience*) [u1]*I had heard that when lamps are put out in the village, the flames gather* *in some remote place and spend the night together, gossiping. So this is where they gather! (*[sd2] *A new Flame enters and is enthusiastically greeted.)'*

The Man's narration '*To the audience'* generates some non-verbal expressions like the proxemic action of the new Flame's entry, and the non-verbal expression of the other Flames to welcome the new Flame. These non-verbal expressions perform the perlocutionary functions because they take place as the effects of the Man's narration. However, the same expressions also have an illocutionary function, as they operate as an enactment 'in' conveying the author's address '*To the audience'*. Thus, the same non-verbal expressions by the Flames have the multiple functions. **The acts are perlocutionary at the interpersonal level of communication** (between the Man and the Flames in this situation); **and the same have the illocutionary functions at the ideational level of communication** (between the author-addresser and all the audiences).

The non-verbal perlocutionary acts and that of the verbal acts are found in a holistic operation. In *Evam Indrajit*, the acts of the 'four spectators', initially (their verbal act of) confirming what they have heard, and eventually (their non-verbal act of) heading towards the stage, are the perlocutions to the act of the Writer's appeal to them to come on the stage. In the same play, it is found that **the playwright's illocution in his non-speech act evolves the characters' non-verbal perlocutionary act,** e.g. *'The Writer becomes the boss and strides in. The three half rise and then sit down scratching their heads.'*

The acts of 'striding in, half rising, sitting down and scratching their heads' are perlocutionary to the playwright's (illocutionary) non-speech acts (of allotting these acts to the characters) 'in' communicating his message to the audiences.

The radio plays evolve the strength of using 'silence', e.g. the silence in p_1 and p_2 below.

MUNSWAMY: (^{sd5}*chuckling*) '(^{sd6}*Rustle of paper.*
   Pause $_{p1}$.)

^{u6} *Madam, if you don't mind me saying, why is a lady from a respectable family like yourself . . . . $_{p2}$?'*

Uma's silence (on Munswamy's sarcastic comment on *hijra*) makes Munswamy pause twice. The illocutionary force in Uma's silence causes Munswamy's perlocution of silence.

The radio plays also prove the strength of the paralinguistic expressions. The paralinguistic response of *'chuckling'* in [sd5] above operates as a non-verbal perlocutionary expression.

The radio plays show also certain **limitation in using the kinesic as well as the proxemic expressions**. **However, certain attempts of establishing the kinesic and the proxemic expressions through the use of music cannot be ignored**, e.g. the *'tinkle of bells'* establishes the actions at *'Champa's house'*; and so does the *'whirring of fan'* with *'the office of the superintendent of police.'*

With the above conclusions, the discussion on the general as well as the component-specific conclusions in the thesis sums up here. The pedagogical implications of the research and the future possibilities of the research in this area are discussed below:

6.4 Pedagogical implications

The present research specified to the speech situations in the print form of drama, implies some pedagogically significant factors at the undergraduate and the postgraduate levels, where drama is prescribed usually in the print form and not in the non-print form. Thus, the pedagogical scope and relevance of the present research begins right at the level of the curriculum design.

The analytical model evolved in the thesis can prove to be a very relevant pedagogical tool. It is certainly useful in the literary studies in the teaching of drama, and also in the linguistic studies to teach pragmatics in general and the literary pragmatics in particular.

It is observed that the activities in the teaching and learning of drama, mainly concentrate on the elements of drama like the theme, the plot, the characterization, the setting etc., and the linguistic analysis of the plays remains a little ignored. It is also observed that even though the plays are analyzed linguistically, the areas like the stage directions, which are a major source of studying the non-verbal communication in drama, are normally not much paid attention to, as much the dialogues in drama are focused on.

The research proves how stage directions matter in the study of drama. In this sense, it opens up certain new pedagogical dimensions in the study of drama as a form of literature. Besides the stage directions, there are a number of other elements, which prove to be significant in the study of drama.

The pragmatic perspective adopted here facilitates a well-knit study of the speech situations, which are processed in the multivalent contexts of the performing and the composite art form of drama. The pragmatic study provides certain analytical tools, without which certain components of the speech situations in drama may not be assessed so properly. For instance, the use of the kinesic, the paralinguistic and the proxemic actions in the non-verbal communication; and also the music, the light effects, the special costumes, the stage property and the likes, which although stand certain pedagogical challenges while studying them in the print form of drama, the same can be objectively assessed even in the print form by using the pragmatic approach adopted in the thesis. The study of speech situations from the phonological perspective can help create awareness among learners as to how utterances acquire new dimensions which not only add to the pragmatics of a given dialogue but also enrich its semantic complexity.

The research is, thus, significant also from the pedagogical point of view.

6.5 Future possibilities of research

The topic of the present research, being part of the multi-dimensional area of drama, and being studied with the process-oriented pragmatic perspective, remains open-ended and opens many a future possibility of research.

As the present study explores the speech situations in the print form, the same way the speech situations in the non-print form, e.g. the theatrical performance, the recorded audio-visual performance, the radio performance and so on, can be explored.

The analytical model evolved here can be further modified to satisfy certain medium-specific analytical requirements, while exploring the aforesaid performances in the non-print form. Such a need-based modification of the analytical model can be a very vital research in itself.

The study can further be narrowed down to specifically focus upon the speech situations from the types of drama like the street plays, the pantomimes (here, particularly the non-verbally communicational situations are analyzable.), the performances in the 'third theatre' or the *'anganmancha'* literally the court-yard stage (see Raha in Anandlal, 2004: 495), so on and so forth.

6.6 Conclusion

The chapter offers an overview of the operational mechanism of the speech situations in drama, enumerating the minute details of the same mechanism, studied in a component-wise sequence.

To sum up, the concept of the speech situations in drama remains open-ended, and so does this study. The book offers a definite basis for the further research. The multiple dimensions of the present topic open up the multiple possibilities for the research in future.

NOTES

Chapter-1

[1] **Components of communication:** the various components of communication mentioned in *Developing Communication Skills* (Mohan & Banerji: 1990).

[2] **Worlds:** the term refers to the worlds in the 'Three World Theory' by Popper (Popper: 1972) and also to the extended 'Fourth World' (Leech: 1983: 52)

[3] **Ideational communication:** Halliday's (1970 and 1973) concept of the ideational function of language, as referred to in *Principles of Pragmatics* (Leech 1983: 56).

Chapter-2

[1] ***Rasa-bhava:*** The communicational roles of the *rasas* and the *bhavas*, stated in the traditional Indian aesthetic theory of '*Rasa-bhava*' in Bharata's *Natyashastra*. See *The Oxford Companion to Indian Theatre* (ed. Anandlal: 2004: 61-62, 414-420).

[2] **Spoken word:** the term refers to Gordon Craig's (1911) view on the dialogue delivery, as elaborated in his *On the Art of the Theatre* (Craig: 1911).

Chapter-3

1. **Socio-pragmatics:** The branch of 'General pragmatics' (Leech: 1983: 11), as referred to in *Principles of Pragmatics* by Leech (1983)

2. **Textual Pragmatics:** The theory of the various 'pragmatic principles and the maxims' (Leech: 1983: 63-70) operating in the textual form of language, as discussed by Leech (1983)

3. **Literary Pragmatics:** The theory that elaborates on the role of 'the author, the narrator, and the reader in the textual mechanisms, and also on the reading as a pragmatic act' (Mey: 1993: 236-261) in *Pragmatics An Introduction* (Mey: 1993)

Chapter-4

1. **Author-addresser:** the author of drama.

2. **Performing-addressers:** the actors in the performance of drama.

3. **Reader-addressees:** the readers of drama.

4. **Viewer-addressees:** the spectators watching drama in the theatre.

5. **Tele-viewer-addressees:** the audience of the tele-visual performance of drama.

6. **Audio-addressees:** the audience of the radio-performance of drama.

7. **Performer-addressees:** all the performers (actors, directors, technicians, and even make-up-man, prompter, back-stage artists, and so on), who read drama for its performance.

Chapter-5

[1] **Sutradhara**: literally 'thread-holder', a central character in Sanskrit theatre and head of the troupe, analogues to a modern director, stage manager, and producer. Some scholars argue that the term originated in ancient puppetry in a very literal sense as 'string-puller' (see *The Oxford Companion to Indian Theatre: 2004: 457*).

[2] **Nandi**: an Indian theatrical convention of invocation to gods and goddesses for the success of the play (see *The Oxford Companion to Indian Theatre*, 2004: 301).

[3] **Purvaranga**: the preliminaries in Sanskrit theatre and later traditional forms, conducted before the commencement of the matter of the main drama (see *The Oxford Companion to Indian Theatre*, 2004: 368).

[4] **Padas**: here referred to as the poetic lines—8 or 12 in number—from *nandi* (see *The Oxford Companion to Indian Theatre*, 2004: 301)

[5] **Sthapaka**: the director or the *sutradhara* (see *The Oxford Companion to Indian Theatre*, 2004: 301)

BIBLIOGRAPHY

1. Abrams M.H. 1957. *A Glossary of Literary Terms*. Madras: Macmillan India Press.

2. Adams J. 1985. *Pragmatics and Fiction*. Amsterdam: John Benjamins Publishing Company.

3. Alekar S. 1989. *The Dread Departure*. Trans. Deshpande Gauri. Calcutta: Seagull Books.

4. Anandlal. 2004. Ed. *The Oxford Companion to Indian Theatre*. New Delhi: Oxford University Press.

5. Armstrong D. Stokoe W. & Wilcox S. 1995. *Gesture and the Nature of Language*. New York: Cambridge University Press.

6. Austin J.L. 1962. *How to Do Things with Words*. London: OUP.

7. Berthold M. 1999. *The History of World Theatre*. New York: Continuum.

8. Bhalla N. 2000. Ed. *Ghashiram Kotwal: Essays and Annotations*. Delhi: Worldview Publications.

9. Birdwhistell R.L. 1952. *Introduction to Kinesics: An Annotation System for Analysis of Body Motion and Gesture*. Washington D.C.: University Microfilms.

10. Brown J.R. 1972. *Theatre Language*. London: The Penguin Press.

11. Burton D. 1980. *Dailogue and Discourse*. London: Routledge & Kegan Paul.

12. Butcher S.H. 1951. *Aristotle's Theory of Poetry and Fine Art*. New York: Dover Publications Inc.

13. Chandler D. 2002. *Semiotics: The Basics*. London: Routledge.

14. Chandra S. 2003-04. 'Vijay Tendulkar's *Kanyadan* Through Reader Response Framework', pp. 232—239 in Dhawan R.K. Ed. *The Indian Journal of English Studies*, Vol. XLI. Delhi: Chaman Offset Press.

15. Cobley P. 2001. Ed. *The Routledge Companion to Semiotics and Linguistics*. London and New York: Routledge.

16. Cook G. 1989. *Discourse*. Oxford: Oxford University Press.

17. Cook G. 1994. *Discourse and Literature*. Oxford: Oxford University Press.

18. Craig E.G. 1911. *On the Art of the Theatre*. London: William Heinemann Ltd.

19. Crystal D. 1980. *A Dictionary of Linguistics and Phonetics*. Malden: Blackwell Publishing Ltd.

20. Cutting J. 2002. *Pragmatics and Discourse*. Routledge.

21. Das Gupta H. N. 1988. *The Indian Theatre*. Delhi: Gian Publishing House.

22. Dattani M. 2000. *Collected Plays*. New Delhi: Penguin Books Ltd.

23. Devi Lal S. Seltmann F. Helstien M. Contractor M.R. 1982. *Our Cultural Fabric*. New Delhi: Ministry of Education and Culture, Govt. of India.

24. Dharwadkar A. 2005. *Theatres of Independence*. New Delhi: Oxford University Press.

25. Duckworth G.E. 1942. Ed. *The Complete Roman Drama*. New York: Random House.

26. Dwivedi A.N. 1999. *Studies in Contemporary Indian English Drama*. Ludhiyana: Kalyani Publishers.

27. Earnest W.B. Hess-Luttich. 1991. 'How Does the Writer of a Dramatic Text Interact With His Audiences?' pp. 225-241, in Sell R.D. Ed. *Literary Pragmatics*. London and New York: Routledge.

28. Evans D.A. 1985. *Situations and Speech Acts: Toward A Formal Semantics of Discourse.* New York & London: Garland Publishing, Inc.

29. Fann K.T. 1969. Ed. *Symposium on J.L. Austin.* London: Routledge & Kegan Paul.

30. Gassner J. 1940. *Masters of the Drama*. New York: Dover Publications, Inc.

31. Gorky M. 1986. *Maxim Gorky Natake*. Trans. Hawaldar A. Mumbai: Lokwangmay Griha Pvt. Ltd.

32. Grice H.P. 1961. 'The Casual Theory of Perception', pp.121-52 in *Proceedings of the Aristotelian Society, Supplementary Volume 35.*

33. Grice H.P. 1967. *Logic and Conversation*. 'The William James lectures'. Published as part-1 of Grice. 1989. Harvard University Press.

34. Grice H.P. 1989. *Studies in the Way of Words*. Cambridge MA: Harvard University Press.

35. Grundy P. 2000. *Doing Pragmatics*. London: Arnold.

36. Gupta B. 1993. *Dramatic Concepts, Greek & Indian*. New Delhi: D.K. Printworld (p) Ltd.

37. Hall Edward. 1966. *The Hidden Dimension*. New York: Doubleday.

38. Halliday M.A.K. 1970. 'Clause Types and Structural Functions', pp. 140-165 in Lyons J. Ed. *New Horizons in Linguistics*. Harmondsworth: Penguin.

39. Halliday M.A.K. 1973. *Explorations in the Functions of Language*. London: Edward Arnold.

40. Halliday M.A.K. and Hasan R. 1985. *Language, Context, and Text: Aspects of Language in a Social-Semiotic Perspective*. Hong Kong: Oxford University Press.

41. Hickey L. 1990. Ed. *The Pragmatics of Style*. London: Routledge.

42. Hickey L. 1998. Ed. *The Pragmatics of Translation*. Clevendon: Cromwell Press Ltd.

43. Hymes D. 1972. 'Models of the Interaction of Language and Social Life' pp. 35-71 in Gumperz and Hymes. 1972. Ed. *Directions in Sociolinguistics*. New York: Holt, Rinehart and Winston, Inc.

44. Jacobs W.W. 'The Monkey's Paw' pp. 193-211 in Oxford, 1998. Ed. *Poetry and Minor Forms of English Literature*. Chennai: OUP.

45. Jakobson R. 1960. *Closing Statement: The Basics*. London: Routledge.

46. Jakobson and Halle. 1956. *Fundamentals of Language*. Mouton: The Hague.

47. Jaworski A. & Coupland N. 1999. *The Discourse Reader*. London and New York: Routledge.

48. Kachru B. 1982. Ed. *The Other Tongue*. Oxford: Oxford University Press.

49. Kangale R.P. 1973. Trans. *Rasa-Bhava-Vichar*. Mumbai: Maharashtra Rajya Sahitya-Sanskriti Mandala.

50. Karnad G., Sircar B. & Tendulkar V. 1989. *Three Modern Indian Plays*. New Delhi: Oxford University Press.

51. Karnad G. 1990. *Naga-Mandala*. New Delhi, India: Oxford University Press.

52. Keir E. 1980. *The Semiotics of Theatre and Drama*. London: Methuen & Co. Ltd.

53. Ketkar G. 1929. *Bharatmuninche Natyashastra*. Mumbai: Popular Prakashan.

54. Kennedy A. 1975. *Six Dramatists in search of a Language*. London: Cambridge University Press.

55. Key Mary R. 1975. *Paralanguage and Kinesics*. Metuchen: The Scarecrow Press, Inc.

56. Kramsch C. 1998. *Language and Culture*. New York: Oxford University Press.

57. Laurence R. Horn and Ward G. 2004. *The Handbook of Pragmatics*. Malden, USA: Blackwell Publishing.

58. Leech G.N. 1983. *Principles of Pragmatics*. Lancaster: Harlow: Longman.

59. Leech G.N. 1992. 'Pragmatic Principles in Shaw's *You Never Can Tell'* pp. 259—280 in Toolan M. 1992. Ed. *Language, Text and Context*. London: Routledge.

60. Levinson S.C. 1983. *Pragmatics*. Cambridge: Cambridge University Press.

61. Lyons J. 1981. *Language and Linguistics*. New York: Cambridge University Press.

62. Malinowski B. 1935. *The Language of Magic and Gardening*, Vol. II: *Coral Gardens and Their Magic*. Bloomington: Indiana University Press.

63. Merrell F. 1985. *A Semiotic Theory of Texts*. Berlin: Mouton de Gruyter.

64. Mey J.L. 1993. *Pragmatics an Introduction*. Australia: Blackwell Publishing.

65. Mohan K. & Banerji M. 1990. *Developing Communication Skills*. Delhi: Macmillan India Ltd.

66. Morris D. Collett P. Marsh P. O'Shaughnessy M. 1979. *Gestures*. London: Jonathan Cape.

67. Naik R. 2003. *Khel Natakacha*. Mumbai: Akshar Prakashan.

68. Osborne J. 1964. *Tom Jones A Film Script*. London: Faber and Faber.

69. Patil N. 2004. 'Speech Situation' pp. 7-15 in Patil L. 2004. Ed. *Dnyanasarita*. Pune: Shriram Offset Printers.

70. Pease A. 1998. *Body Language*. London: Sheldon Press.

71. Popper K.R. 1972. *Objective Knowledge: An Evolutionary Approach*. Oxford: The Clarendon Press.

72. Posner R. 1985. pp. 231 in Earnest W.B. Hess-Luttich. 1991. 'How Does the Writer of a Dramatic Text Interact With His Audiences?' pp. 225-241 in Sell R.D. 1991. Ed. *Literary Pragmatics*. London and New York: Routledge.

73. Poole S.C. 1999. *An Introduction to Linguistics*. London: Palgrave Publishing Ltd.

74. Prakasam V. & Abbi A. 1986. *Semantic Theories and Language Teaching*. New Delhi: Allied Publishers Private Limited.

75. Prakasam V. 2004. 'Towards a Theory of Pragmeme' pp. 81-95 in Kumar A. 2004, Ed. *Language Context and Culture*. Lucknow: Gurukul Publications.

76. Prasad K.S. 2002. *The Philosophy of Language in Classical Indian Tradition*. New Delhi: Decent Books.

77. Saraswathi V. 2006. 'Pragmatic Competence: A Nelected Area', pp. 7-15 in Thorat A. Ed. *Asian Quarterly*, Vol. 4, Issue. 3. Pune: Forum for Culture Studies.

78. Saussure F. 1916/1974. *Course in General Linguistics*. Trans. Baskin W. London: Fontana / Collins.

79. Schiffrin D. Tannen D. & Hamilton H. E. 2001. Ed. *The Handbook of Discourse Analysis*. Malden: Blackwell Publishers.

80. Searle J.R. 1969. *Speech Acts*. London: Cambridge University Press.

81. Searle J.R. 1971. 'What is a Speech Act?' in Searle J.R. Ed. *The Philosophy of Language*. London: OUP.

82. Searle J.R. 1979. 'Indirect Speech Acts', pp. 59-82 in Cole P. and Morgan J.L. Ed. *Speech Acts: Syntax and Semantics*. New York: Academic Press.

83. Sinclair J. 1995. Ed. *Collins Cobuild English Dictionary*. London: Harper Collins Publishers.

84. Sperber and Wilson. 1986a, 1987a, b, 1995, 1998a, 2002, and pp. 607-632 in Laurence R. Horn and Ward G. 2004. Ed. *The Handbook of Pragmatics*. Malden, USA: Blackwell Publishing.

85. Srampickal J. 1994. *Voice to the Voiceless: the Power of People's Theatre in India*. London: Hurst & Company.

86. Stanislavski C. 1981. *Creating a Role*. London: Methuen Publishing Ltd.

87. Stockwell P. 2002. *Sociolinguistics*. London: Routledge.

88. Tendulkar V. 1986. *Ghashiram Kotwal*. Seagull Books. Trans. Karve J. & Zelliot E. 1999. Kolkatta: Seagull.

89. Tendulkar V. 2003. *Ghashiram Kotwal*. pp. 359-416 in *Collected Plays in Translation*. New Delhi: Oxford University Press.

90. Thorat A. 2006. 'Cooperative Principle and Politeness Principle', pp. 97-101 in Thorat A. Ed. *Asian Quarterly*, Vol. 4, Issue. 3. Pune: Forum for Culture Studies.

91. Thorat A. 2006. Ed. *Pragmatics*. Pune: Institute of Advanced Studies in English.

92. Toolan M. 1992. Ed. *Language Text and Context*. London: Routledge.

93. Tripathi K.D. 2004. 'Sanskrit Theatre' pp. 414-420 in Anandlal. 2004. Ed. *The Oxford Companion to Indian Theatre*. New Delhi: Oxford University Press.

94. Van Laan T.F. 1970. *The Idiom of Drama*. Ithaca &London: Cornell University Press.

95. Varadpande M.L. 1978. *Traditions of Indian Theatre*. Delhi: Abhinav Publications.

96. Varadpande M.L. 1983. *Religion and Theatre*. New Delhi: Abhinav Publications.

97. Varadpande M.L. 1987. *History of Indian Theatre*. Delhi: Abhinav Publications.

98. Verschueren Jef. 1999. *Understanding Pragmatics*. London: Arnold.

99. Welmers W.E. 1954. 'Non-segmental elements in foreign language learning', pp.130-36 in Mueller Hugo. 1954. Ed. '*Report of the 5th Annual Round Table Meeting on Linguistics and Language Teaching*'. Washington D.C.: Georgetown University.

100. Woodford K. & Jackson G. 2003. Ed. *Cambridge Advanced Learner's Dictionary*, Version 1.0. Cambridge University Press.

101. Yule G. 1985. *The Study of Language*. Cambridge: Cambridge University Press.

102. Watts R.J. 2003. *Politeness*. Cambridge: Cambridge University Press.

103. Zuber O. 1980. Ed. *The Languages of Theatre*. Oxford: Pergamon Press.